Fathers matter! topics and chap and challenge. fathers our families need and that our Lord intends us to be.

MW01681179

Dr. Rex Horne, former executive director,
Arkansas Baptist State Convention

Fathers Matter covers the role of biblical fatherhood in a great way. Like the old Clint Eastwood movie, the seven chapters share "the good, the bad, and the ugly." I suggest it as an excellent study for fathers today.

Joseph Burt, associational missionary,
Red River Baptist Association

Fathers Matter: The Bible Tells Us So reminds us of the crucial role fathers play in modeling behavior for their children and family. This is a necessary reminder of this important biblical role and why it matters.

Bobby Thomas, president/CEO,
Arkansas Baptist Foundation

Illuminated by Scripture and illustrated with real-life stories, this book convicts and inspires the reader to pursue becoming the kind of father that truly matters.

Dr. Ben Sells, president,
Ouachita Baptist University

Fathers Matter

Fathers Matter

The Bible Tells Us So

GREAT COMMISSION
BAPTIST ASSOCIATION

Fathers Matter: The Bible Tells Us So
Copyright © 2025 by Great Commission Baptist Association.
All rights reserved.

Unless otherwise marked, Scripture quotations are taken from the Christian Standard Bible®, copyright © 2017 by Holman Bible Publishers. Used by permission. Christian Standard Bible® and CSB® are federally registered trademarks of Holman Bible Publishers.

Scripture quotations marked (ESV) are from the ESV® Bible (the Holy Bible, English Standard Version®), © 2001 by Crossway, a publishing ministry of Good News Publishers. Used by permission. All rights reserved.

ISBN: 978-1-964895-10-9

Contents

Preface

In October 2023, I ran into the executive director of Arkansas Baptist Children and Family Ministries, Derek Brown, in the exhibit hall of the Arkansas Baptist State Convention's annual meeting. He shared an observation with me concerning the crisis of fatherlessness this generation is facing. He said, "Jeff, the last time I did a Google search on how to be a good father, the first few pages that came up were government websites. It seems like the government recognizes the problem and is providing more resources to help men be good fathers than the church is. That's not right."

We agreed it was a shame but quickly moved on to more pressing realities.

Over the next few weeks, I couldn't get Derek's comment out of my head. It haunted me. At first, I thought he must be exaggerating, but when I ran a Google search on this topic, I saw that he was right. In addition to government websites, many books on biblical manhood also exist—and some dedicate a chapter or two to fatherhood. If you run that same Google search today, you will find a number of nonprofit and faith-based sites that provide articles or book recommendations addressing the topic of fatherhood. We rejoice in that reality.

At the same time, it's concerning to me that Baptists—particularly Arkansas Baptists—have not made much contribution to the cause. And how ironic: While Arkansas Baptists believe that helping men become godly, biblical fathers is important, it seems to be less urgent than other pressing matters. In the spring of 2024, I concluded that the Lord was making it urgent to me.

And God's timing was perfect. During this time, I was watching my two sons become godly fathers to my young grandchildren. Simultaneously, I was seeing a positive shift in the Baptist Church: More and more young fathers were bringing their children to church—and to the activities and events our churches provide for families.

I approached the Great Commission Baptist Association with a modest proposal: to compile a short book written by representatives of our Arkansas Baptist agencies to illustrate what the Bible says about fatherhood. We agreed this project was important and that the Lord had given us the vision to see it accomplished.

The book you hold in your hands is the result of that vision. While we believe that one of the ways God speaks is through general revelation and that many resources are available that generally address God's design for fathers, we also believe that God speaks most clearly through His Word. That's why we asked each of the authors in this book to choose a specific passage or recurring theme from Scripture as the foundation for their chapter. We are trusting the promise of Isaiah 55:11: that God's Word "will not return to [Him] empty" but "will prosper in what [He sends] it to do."

Baptists are at their best when they work together. For that reason, it was important to include different stories that address the topic of fatherhood from the lives of Arkansas Baptists and the lives of our authors who are all Arkansas Baptist fathers.

God provided seven godly men who collectively represent the entirety of Arkansas Baptist life. Here is the range of the wisdom the Lord provided for this volume:

- Chapter 1, "Raising Disciples: A Father's Lifelong Task" (Bill Elliff), plumbs the depths of Genesis 22.
- Chapter 2, "The Way of Grace for Fathers" (James Barham), explains how the gospel message of God's grace heals our relationships from the devastation of the Fall.
- Chapter 3, "What It Means to Be a Man" (Tim Noel), helps us grasp the fatherly wisdom that King David passed on to his son Solomon in 1 Kings 2.
- Chapter 4, "Words from the Father: Three Things Every Child Needs to Hear" (Jeff Thompson), focuses on Matthew 17, detailing how the words of God the Father to His Son, Jesus, serve as a model for how earthly fathers should encourage their children.
- Chapter 5, "How to Be a Bad Dad" (Craig Jenkins), explores Lot's life in Genesis 19, identifying mistakes every father should seek to avoid.
- Chapter 6, "Dads Make a Difference" (Bobby Clark), examines Mordecai as a father figure in Esther's life and how God sometimes uses men who are not a child's father to fill the fatherhood gap.

- Chapter 7, "Fulfilling Our Role as Fathers" (Travis McCormick), illustrates what it looks like for a 21st-century father to live out Proverbs 22:6.

This book was written as a resource for the churches of Arkansas. We hope that it will be shared with fathers, that it will serve as a guide for discussions in men's groups, that it will be the seeds of better sermons on these passages, and that it will bless families throughout Arkansas in ways we cannot imagine. It is our humble prayer that God will use this book to communicate His truth and strengthen fathers across our state—and even beyond.

We want to thank the editors of Good Comma Editing, whose faithful work helps pastors and preachers "state the most important things clearly" by weaving sermons and Bible studies into coherent books. We couldn't have done it without them. We also want to thank the Great Commission Baptist Association for underwriting this project. Any proceeds from this book will go to the Fatherhood Project, a fund with the Arkansas Baptist Foundation, to be used to strengthen fathers across our state in coordination with Arkansas Baptist Children and Family Ministries and the Great Commission Baptist Association.

Jeff Thompson
Associational Missions Strategist
Great Commission Baptist Association

1

Raising Disciples: A Father's Lifelong Task

BILL ELLIFF

Paul Davis was a tough man. In the late 1930s, he became the light heavyweight boxing champion for the Navy's Seventh Fleet. But Davis's toughness came at a high cost: His dad had been killed in action as a motorcycle policeman. Paul was fueled by an underlying caldron of hurt and anger. Growing up without his father's influence had hardened him.

After the war, Paul married and had three children. He also had a drinking problem that led to divorce. The tragic result was that Paul's young children would grow up in the same way—without the daily influence of their father.

Paul's oldest child, Stephen, was just six years old when his parents divorced. Like his dad, Stephen made a name for himself as an athlete. Heading into college, he had earned a spot in the lineup on The University of Oklahoma baseball team. His collegiate success also opened several professional doors for him. Ultimately, he decided to go to Hollywood to try to make a name for himself as an actor. In time, he found himself empty and desperately crying out to God.

As unlikely as it may sound, Stephen grabbed the yellow pages and—by God's grace—found his way to a church filled with people who knew the Lord. They led him to Christ and began to disciple him. God put him on a fast track of spiritual development. When the time was right, God even called him to preach. He got a seminary education, married his wonderful wife, Jonya, and had three children in their early years of ministry.[1]

Discipleship at Church

As a young pastor, Stephen established an early morning men's discipleship ministry in his congregation. But the Lord whispered to him, "Stephen, your first group of disciples is at home. Start there." He realized he needed to train his own kids—to give them the spiritual foundation he had never received from his father. But growing up in a fatherless home had left him clueless about how to raise his kids to love and fear the Lord. He and Jonya started by reading Scripture with their kids, making it a daily habit.

Stephen sensed they needed a method for pouring Scripture into their kids. So he leaned into his baseball background and created a morning routine called "Bible Baseball." Every morning, the Davis family went around the table and recited Scripture. They would "go around the bases" by each reciting their verses to get "home" in order to start their breakfast. It was a fun way for their family to learn to love God and His Word. And it led to a lifelong program of discipleship. Stephen, a 27-year pastor of First Baptist Church in Russellville, Arkansas, and Jonya have raised three of the godliest kids you could imagine—kids who, now that they're grown, are discipling the next generation.

Stephen and Jonya changed their family tree, raising children who all serve the Lord.[2]

Our Intentional Creator

One of the lessons we can learn from Stephen's story is that God knows what He is doing. He is precise in His providence and created each person according to His design. The Bible says that He knitted us together in our mother's womb (Psalm 139:13). We were made like Him, in His image, so that we could join Him in His redemptive work, which includes raising godly children who follow Him.

Just as God knew who your parents would be, He also knew that you would become a parent, establishing you as the father of your children. He designed you—with all your strengths and weaknesses—to be the dad to *your* kids. From God's perspective, no one could fulfill this role for your kids better than you. But just like any calling from God, you must cooperate with the Lord if you want to raise godly children. You won't simply wake up in 20 years and magically have kids who love Him. If you leave your children unattended, the devil will try to pull them into darkness.

As a father, you must commit yourself to intentionally mentoring your children in the things of God. Discipleship will protect them from the one who longs "to steal and kill and destroy" (John 10:10). As a father, this is your first and greatest priority.

Our Models and Our Manual

As always, God provides us with the necessary resources to accomplish the task He has assigned to us. The Word of God and His Spirit are available for us if we will come with hungry hearts and a passion to train our children, looking to God as our powerful and perfect fatherhood coach.

Scripture provides many examples of men who serve as models for godly fatherhood. Some of the lessons these fathers provide come from their missteps. For example, Eli struck out with his own sons. David committed multiple errors and let his son Absalom run wild. But other lessons come from fathers who, though far from perfect, raised great sons and daughters.

One of these Hall of Famers is Abraham, the father of faith. His championship play comes into focus through one powerful scene recorded in Genesis 22. This chapter is full of lessons that apply even today. The story begins decades earlier when Abraham and Sarah prayed for a son. It wasn't until Abraham was 100 years old that Isaac was born! But when Isaac was a young teenager, God approached Abraham with a strange command:

> "Take your son," he said, "your only son Isaac, whom you love, go to the land of Moriah, and offer him there as a burnt offering on one of the mountains I will tell you about." (Genesis 22:2)

What a test of his faith! God was sending Abraham to Mount Moriah—the place where God would offer His own Son as a sacrifice—where Jesus would eventually be crucified. God was asking Abraham, the father who had waited so long for a son, to sacrifice Isaac to the Lord. You and I know how the story turns out, but we can still imagine the way Abraham and Isaac must have felt. This was the ultimate test for Abraham and his son. It stands as one of the most pivotal moments in Old Testament history.

But buried in this one scene are several powerful and practical lessons that fathers can use as a manual for discipleship. Let's walk up the mountain with Abraham and Isaac and examine seven life-changing ways to disciple our children.

Seven Life-Changing Ways to Disciple Your Children

1. PRAY UNCEASINGLY

Long before Abraham came on the scene, God had planned to give him a son. In a prayer conversation between God and Abraham, the Lord revealed what He had in mind:

> I will bless those who bless you, I will curse anyone who treats you with contempt, and all the peoples on earth will be blessed through you. (Genesis 12:3)

God made a sacred covenant with Abraham that He would bless not only his family but also the whole world. And it was during another time of prayer that Abraham received his instruction for what to do with Isaac on Mount Moriah. Don't miss this. If Abraham had not been a man of prayer, he would have missed what God had in mind for him and for "all the peoples on earth."

Do you want to know how to lead your children? Then pray. Of all the ways God can communicate with us, His two primary avenues are through His Word and through prayer. The one who knit your children together—the one who knows them best—will instruct you. The perfect Father is eager to share His fatherhood advice with you and through you. Fathers who long to develop their children for Christ must take the first step by becoming men of prayer.

Use whatever means necessary to help you develop a strong rhythm of prayer for your children. You might want to record your prayers in a notebook or journal. The pages will grow as you record God's answers. This handwritten record will be a mighty testimony to your children in the years to come.

Once, as I was praying for my 27 grandkids, I realized that Satan has schemes for all of them. He is seeking to capture their lives for his godless purposes. Bolstered by the prayers of their parents and grandparents, your children will be able to stand strong against the Enemy.

Do you want God's protection for your children? Then pray! Paul reminds us in Ephesians 6:10–18 that we're battling for their hearts, minds, and souls. We must understand the severity of the battle, put on the full armor of God, and then stay alert by doing one foundational task:

> Pray at all times in the Spirit with every prayer and request, and stay alert with all perseverance and intercession for all the saints. (Ephesians 6:18)

Without prayer, we have only ourselves to rely on. With prayer, we have God to rely on for the protection of our children. Nothing brings God into the lives of our children as powerfully and directly as consistent prayer.

2. BELIEVE FAITHFULLY

The foundation of our spiritual lives is faith. The Bible teaches that "without faith it is impossible to please God" (Hebrews 11:6). Abraham's crisis moment in Genesis 22 teaches us the importance of depending on every word that comes from the mouth of God. Take a moment to consider Abraham's unquestioning obedience to God's instructions as proof of his mature faith:

> So Abraham got up early in the morning, saddled his donkey, and took with him two of his young men and his son Isaac. (Genesis 22:3)

Think of what Abraham's faith—all the way to lifting the knife to slay Isaac—taught his son. Abraham's willingness to believe God, even against all logic, became a lifelong lesson for Isaac: God can be trusted, and He will faithfully provide.

From his moments of conversation with God, Abraham learned that God reveals Himself to people of prayer. Abraham shared with Isaac his faith in God to provide:

> Then Isaac spoke to his father Abraham and said, "My father." And he replied, "Here I am, my son." Isaac said, "The fire and the wood are here, but where is the lamb for the burnt offering?" Abraham answered, "God himself will provide the lamb for the burnt offering, my son." (Genesis 22:7–8)

I can relate to this. My mother believed that God spoke to her through the 7,000 promises recorded in the Bible and that she could take Him at His word. In the margins of her Bible, she wrote my name and the names of my siblings next to specific life promises that she believed for us. It is uncanny how specifically God has fulfilled those promises.

I applied this lesson from my mom when one of my sons strayed into a time of some teenage rebellion. At a particularly excruciating moment, I asked God to give me a promise for my son so I could know how to pray in faith for him. The next morning, in my normal Bible reading, this passage jumped off the page:

> All your sons will be taught of the Lord; and the well-being of your sons will be great. (Isaiah 54:13 NASB 1995)

I began to pray that verse daily—that the Lord would teach my son and that his "well-being would be great." Six months later, he showed up broken and repentant. He is now in his 30s, married with four children, and is discipling them to love the Lord. He is a godly, passionate follower of Christ!

All four of my kids have had conversations like the following with me when they are struggling. For example, they might say, "I don't know what to do about this, Dad." I then ask a question they have heard me ask before: "You know what this is about, right?" "Yes," they'll reply. "It's about God teaching me to trust Him, isn't it?" And I'll respond by saying, "Absolutely. What do you think God is saying? How do you think He wants you to trust Him in this situation?"

Conversations like this teach us to trust the ever-faithful one together. Most often, my kids walk away with a new perspective. What they originally viewed as an overwhelming problem they now see as an opportunity for faith.

Manley Beasley, one of my mentors, used to say, "Needs are God's messenger boys, telling us He has an answer."

What are you believing God about for your children? Are you discipling them through times of need to be men and women who put their faith in God?

3. WALK CLOSELY

If you read the familiar story of Abraham and Isaac too quickly, you will miss an important detail that occurs between the statements "The two of them walked on together . . ." and "When they arrived at the place . . ." Read the verses below and think about what occurs in between:

> Abraham answered, "God himself will provide the lamb for the burnt offering, my son." Then the two of them walked on together. When they arrived at the place that God had told him about, Abraham built the altar there and arranged the wood. (Genesis 22:8–9)

How long is the gap between walking on together and arriving at the destination? Think about what may have occurred between Abraham and Isaac as they walked.

Walking with someone is powerful. Walking clears the mind and gives ample time for real conversation. And walking *takes us somewhere*. It's the God-given means to get you from where you are to wherever God needs you to go.

Walking with your children provides an essential ingredient for discipleship: time. Discipleship is a significant time commitment. Some of the time you spend will be focused and instructive, while some will be unhurried and relaxed.

Jesus had just three years to disciple His "kids." Ponder the methods He used as He equipped His 12 world changers. One profound example of this is found in Mark 3:14–15:

> He appointed twelve, whom he also named apostles, to be with him, to send them out to preach, and to have authority to drive out demons.

These men became *like* Him because they were *with* Him. They learned how to deal with people by watching Him love a Samaritan woman. They observed how He responded to His critics. They understood how to respect the government by seeing Him pay His taxes. They found out how they were to live with spiritual power by observing the intensity of His prayer life. The observational lessons occurred because Jesus spent time with them. Lots of time.

Discipling your kids requires your physical presence; it takes an investment of time, over time. That means you need to prioritize time with them just as you prioritize a professional appointment. Prioritize time at the beginning and the end of your workday. Honor special family days. Take time for family vacations. Memory-making getaways are like pure gold. It will be worth all the planning and money you spend in the long run.

In addition, plan one-on-one dates with your children. "Dating" each of my eight children individually became normal as they were growing up. At the beginning of each week, they would talk about whose turn it was to "go on a date with Dad." Our Dad dates were far from elaborate; sometimes it simply meant going to the store together for a treat.

We were doing what Abraham and Isaac did between "The two of them walked on together . . ." and "When they arrived at the place . . ." We were taking time to be together, but as we "walked together," we talked. I learned the art of asking questions. Sometimes, I gave advice, but mostly, I simply listened.

Jesus used His time with the disciples to equip them, to communicate the Word to them, and to teach them how to have spiritual authority over the Enemy. But much of what Jesus did with the disciples involved everyday things: They ate meals together, they fished together, and they walked together. We can learn from Jesus's example. There are times when we need to have "teachable moments" with our kids, but we win an audience for those moments simply by spending time with them on everyday things and getting to know them—thereby gaining their friendship in order to disciple fruitfully. Because each child is different, we need to spend one-on-one time with them in order to learn about and discern their unique needs.

Parents obviously shouldn't just be friends with their kids, but being their friend—walking with them, talking with them, and getting to know them—is important. My wife and I discovered that walking with our children in love covers a multitude of parenting failures. We always worked hard to win their hearts.

Don't merely speculate about how much time you spend with your kids. Instead, record the minutes over the course of a month. And be honest. If you need to prioritize them more effectively, then do so. No dad will ever say on his deathbed, "I wish I'd spent more time at work!"

4. TEACH COMPREHENSIVELY

Long before Abraham and Sarah became parents, God let Abraham know that He planned on building a nation of people through their lineage. God intended to know and walk with His people, and as part of this plan, He instructed parents to own the responsibility of instilling God's Word in their children. There could be no greater way for a nation to be developed in the ways of God—not through a school or a class—than for parents to instruct their children during the normal rhythms of everyday life. Scripture conveys the pattern like this:

> These words that I am giving you today are to be in your heart. Repeat them to your children. Talk about them when you sit in your house and when you walk along the road, when you lie down and when you get up. (Deuteronomy 6:6–7)

Helping our children learn from every teachable moment does not need to be a classroom lecture, but every moment *does* contain a lesson we can share with them! To do this well, we must first walk with God ourselves. Then we should talk to Him about what is happening in our lives and in our children's lives, praying that they will be able to see His purposes. Here are some examples of how natural this can become:

- While on a trip, stop at a beautiful spot and say, "Hey kids, look at those mountains! Who do you think made those? Why does God give us mountains? What do they say to us about Him?"

- Pause during a tough moment of discipline and help them see the situation through God's eyes. Take the time to explain why this correction is so important, saying, "If we don't help you learn how to be obedient to the authorities God places in your life, you may find it hard to be responsive to God's authority when He seeks to lead you. Does that make sense?"
- Give thanks at every meal, repeatedly acknowledging God's gracious provisions. Don't say perfunctory, cliché prayers but invite your children to lead in prayer and teach them to pray with gratitude.
- Teach them from an early age to tithe—and to give spontaneously out of generous hearts and from the understanding that we are joyful stewards of God's resources.

When Abraham was asked a question by his son, he responded with a biblical truth: "God himself will provide the lamb" (Genesis 22:8). He related the moment to the reality of God's presence and provision for their lives. He taught his son something about God that applied to this moment.

Make discipleship more than "a lecture from Dad" at every turn. Let your children feel that their father is so interested in them that he is instructing them about life. In this way, they will learn to believe that all truth is God's truth and that God wants His children to see and glorify Him in everything.

A parent's primary discipleship window stays open for about 18 years. We should take a lesson from Jesus's three years with His disciples. He identified the primary truths He wanted them to know and then taught these truths to them. We should prioritize those truths to our kids as we sit and walk along the road together and when we lie down each night and get up each morning (Deuteronomy 6:7). There should be times of formal instruction, but it must be reinforced by helping our children see that all of life is about God and His ways. They need to know that we were made like Him so that we could join Him in His work.

5. WORSHIP FERVENTLY

In Abraham's journey up the mountain, he eventually tells his servants that he and Isaac will go on ahead without them:

> Then Abraham said to his young men, "Stay here with the donkey. The boy and I will go over there to worship; then we'll come back to you." (Genesis 22:5)

Abraham wasn't being deceitful when he said, "We'll come back to you." He wasn't giving a hypocritical, super-spiritual answer either. Abraham was prepared to worship. He had gathered what was needed: the wood, the fire, and a knife. He had even traveled to Mount Moriah, where God had told him to worship. Abraham intentionally took Isaac with him, per God's instruction, so he could worship too. The father of faith believed that the purpose of this sacred moment on the mountain was going to be a powerful act of worship.

Men—sometimes more than women—tend to marginalize worship. Some men might say, "Well, I'm not much of a singer, so worship is not my deal." That statement is understandable because we've often reduced worship to the singing part of a church service. But a man who understands the need to build his children into fully devoted followers of Jesus Christ must gain an understanding of true worship.

Worship is understanding who God is and giving Him the honor and praise He deserves. (Read that again and think about it carefully.)

Worship should stand as one of our greatest passions. Worship should become our priority in every act of every day. And we must teach this to our kids as well.

Abraham knew the trip up the mountain was going to teach his son about who God was. What Abraham did not know was just how great an encounter it would be! Together, father and son were about to encounter El Shaddai—God Almighty. They were on the cusp of encountering Jehovah Jireh—the God who provides. With one hike up a mountain and a bold step of surrender, God would make Himself known.

Take a moment to consider this from Isaac's point of view. In that moment, this young man worshipped God with his whole life laid upon the altar. He had worshipped God before, but he would never forget *this* moment.

Fathers, this is what our kids should see in how we approach worship with them every week, both in church and outside of church. We should be prepared with the supplies for worship, go to the place of worship, and be ready to engage in worship. Our worship should be fervent. Our children should hear us singing often (in worship services and around the house). It matters less about our musical ability and more about our attitude toward God. They should know that we love to praise God regardless of what others think. They should see us praying and studying and listening and responding to God's Word. Let your kids have the lifelong memory of seeing their dad pore over the Scriptures.

Additionally, family worship needs to be a regular routine, whether at the start of the day or just before bedtime. Praying at meals should be an expected norm as well. Recognizing who God is should be something everyone in the house is used to. Stopping to mention God's provision should become as natural as breathing. Praying with each child as you tuck them into bed should be as common as brushing their teeth or putting on their pajamas.

Dads should seek to do daily what Abraham and Isaac did when they went "over there" to worship (Genesis 22:5). What could be more beautiful than developing a humble, grateful son or daughter who knows that in your family, everyone understands who God is and gives Him the glory and praise He deserves.

6. POSITION SPIRITUALLY

Another important lesson from Abraham and Isaac's encounter with God is that Abraham took his son to a setting where he could encounter God.

> When they arrived at the place that God had told him about, Abraham built the altar there and arranged the wood. (Genesis 22:9)

God loves to make Himself known. He created us to know Him and experience His presence. Everything flows from the presence of the Lord. If you have His nearness in your life, whether it be in your home, in your church, or in your ministry, you have everything you need. If you don't, you have nothing that matters or lasts.

But experiencing His presence is a choice. Just ask Mary and Martha about the day Jesus stopped by their home in Bethany. Mary sat at the Lord's feet and learned from Him, while Martha missed Christ's presence because she was overly focused on the details of the day. Here is what He said to her:

> Martha, Martha, you are worried and upset about many things, but one thing is necessary. Mary has made the right choice, and it will not be taken away from her. (Luke 10:41–42)

A dad must also make daily choices to position himself to meet with God: to prioritize worshipping every week at church, to turn off the car radio and spend that time in prayer, to go on the men's retreat, to be at the prayer gathering, and so forth. A committed dad must learn how to draw near to the Lord daily, communing with Him and repenting of sin to remove spiritual barriers. He must learn to abide in Christ. To do this, he must *choose* to be where God is. His children need to see their dad prioritizing being in God's presence on a regular basis. Then he can begin to include his kids in some of these activities, giving them opportunities to be in the presence of Christ—like Abraham did for his son on Mount Moriah. Don't miss this: Abraham took His son to a place where he could encounter God.

> When they arrived at the place that God had told him about, Abraham built the altar there and arranged the wood. (Genesis 22:9)

We can't make our children respond to Christ, but we can put them in optimal environments where worship happens.

I once traveled with a ministry that helped churches experience personal and corporate revival. We took our families with us. God would often show up powerfully—often enough that we could sense when God was going to do some spiritual work among His people.

One night, I took my eight-year-old son out of his normal children's class and had him come sit with me in the adult gathering. The room was pregnant with the presence of God. The Lord began to move. Soon, I heard my son sniffling and then felt a tug on my pant leg. I looked down and he said, "Dad, God is calling me to preach!" and burst into tears. We went to a side room and prayed together. God's calling on my son's future vocation was no surprise to me. Don't get me wrong: I didn't know that God would call my eight-year-old son *that* night. But I sensed God was calling me to have him with me in the adult service. I obeyed God, and He used that moment to put a calling on my son's heart. Thirty years later, he has become a great pastor and a strong leader in a church-planting movement.

When your children want to go to church camp, make every sacrifice to get them there. Get them involved in a good youth group. When you have meetings with godly men and women, include your children so they can hear the wisdom shared. Watch spiritual videos together. If you want to disciple them strongly, position them in the presence of God.

7. SURRENDER COMPLETELY

To walk with God fully means to surrender control fully to Him. You must let Him lead, understanding that He is perfect in His leadership. Life must be about His agenda, not yours. You must yield your plans into God's hands, just as Abraham did with Isaac. What Abraham did as he gave his beloved son—one of the greatest acts of human surrender—was a picture of what God the Father did with Jesus on that same mountain centuries later.

Our children are not our own. They belong to God, and we are stewards in a sacred trust. Abraham was willing to surrender his only son in accordance with God's will. You can feel the seriousness of the scene as father and son walk toward the place of worship:

> Isaac said, "The fire and the wood are here, but where is the lamb for the burnt offering?" Abraham answered, "God himself will provide the lamb for the burnt offering, my son." Then the two of them walked on together. (Genesis 22:7–8)

"God himself will provide the lamb." Charles Spurgeon described a truth that Abraham seemed to understand:

> The worldling blesses God while he gives him plenty, but the Christian blesses him when he smites him: He believes him to be too wise to err

> and too good to be unkind; he trusts him where he cannot trace him, looks up to him in the darkest hour, and believes that all is well.[3]

Scripture makes no mention that Isaac fought Abraham as his father placed him on the altar. Somehow, this young man had been taught to trust God enough that he had come to believe both his earthly father and his heavenly Father. God rewarded the full surrender of both father and son in ways they could never imagine. Catch the full force of God's blessing to Abraham:

> Abraham looked up and saw a ram caught in the thicket by its horns. So Abraham went and took the ram and offered it as a burnt offering in place of his son. And Abraham named that place The LORD Will Provide, so today it is said, "It will be provided on the LORD's mountain." Then the angel of the LORD called to Abraham a second time from heaven and said, "By myself I have sworn," this is the LORD's declaration: "Because you have done this thing and have not withheld your only son, I will indeed bless you and make your offspring as numerous as the stars of the sky and the sand on the seashore. Your offspring will possess the city gates of their enemies. And all the nations of the earth will be blessed by your offspring because you have obeyed my command." (Genesis 22:13–18)

Not only did God provide the lamb, but this father-son duo gave the world a testimony that will glorify God forever.

I was once counseling a young couple who wanted to get married. I began to tell the husband-to-be what marriage would require of him. He was not a follower of Christ. I told him honestly what God called husbands to do—and that he would one day stand before God and give an account.

He sank low into the little couch in my office. Finally, he stopped me and said, "I can't do this without Christ, can I?"

"Of course not," I said. "But you can do all things when you let God take up residence inside you."

I had the privilege in that moment of leading this young man to embrace Christ as his Lord and Savior.

This man's realization about the high calling of being a husband applies to discipling your children as well. Without Christ and His daily presence, you cannot hope to disciple your children. But with Him and His all-powerful presence, you have everything you need to help your kids embrace the purpose God intended for them before they were even created.

Bill Elliff is the founding and National Engage pastor of The Summit Church's family of churches in Arkansas. Bill has authored more than 15 books and numerous articles. He has served in many different facets of Southern Baptist life, most recently serving on the board of trustees of Ouachita Baptist University and helping numerous state conventions in various prayer initiatives. Bill has been married to his wife, Holly, for more than 52 years. They currently have 8 married children and 27 grandchildren!

2

The Way of Grace for Fathers

JAMES BARHAM

The LORD is gracious and compassionate, slow to anger and great in faithful love. (Psalm 145:8)

In Psalm 145:8, the psalmist describes some of God's key attributes. What comes to your mind when you think about God? When I ponder who God is, I think about this verse. Subsequently, I also think about this quote by A. W. Tozer: "The most important thing about you is what you think about when you think about God."[4] Let that sink in for a moment.

As a dad, I want my children to know who God the Father is, and I want them to walk closely with Him every day. For that reason, I share this verse with them daily so it becomes a banner written on their hearts. Long after I am gone, I want them to know just how much God loves them.

Passing on an understanding of God's love is a major part of my role as a father. Let me show you the framework for how I seek to pass these values on to my kids.

Living as Role Models for Our Children

I've had some great male role models. My dad demonstrated strength, provision, and an industrious work ethic. As a farmer, he carried the weight of financial pressures and he handled daily decisions with grace. Then there are my two uncles. Uncle William showed me how to be a steward of land and resources, while Uncle James, a World War II veteran, embodied warmth, acceptance, and a gentle spirit. And my grandfather modeled service in big and small ways. He served in World War II, but in his 90s, he bicycled around our town picking up trash. I am who I am today due to the role models God placed in my early childhood.

Strong role models shape a person's core beliefs as early as age five. Young children are asking, "Who am I?" "What makes adults proud of me?" "What can I do to win approval?" They may not articulate the questions with words, but their values are being solidified in the tender years of childhood. Words that adults speak to them or about them shape how they see themselves as well as who they become.

Uncle James used to say to me, "You're a good man, Charlie Brown." He was really saying, "I'm proud of you!" He also complimented me, saying, "Thanks for helping me out around the house and the garden." His words helped me understand that I had value—and that helping was a good trait. As I got older, his words took on even higher value because I realized he was a man who grew up during the Great Depression and was part of the "Greatest Generation."

Through role models, I have learned the impact my words can have on my children. Words reveal who we are. They come from our character. They overflow from our hearts. We should use Psalm 145:8 as an example of how to speak to our children, remembering that our heavenly Father is "gracious and compassionate, slow to anger and great in faithful love."

As dads, God calls us to encourage our children by reflecting His gracious, compassionate, and patient heart to them. We must teach our sons and daughters who God is, about His ways, and how to obey Him. In order to do this well, we must first know God's character ourselves.

Knowing and Reflecting Our Heavenly Father

The description of God's character from Psalm 145 shows up in several places throughout the Bible. The Holy Spirit inspired many Old Testament writers to reveal who God is throughout the years. For example, David wrote, "The Lord is compassionate and gracious, slow to anger and abounding in faithful love" (Psalm 103:8). You can add Joel's name to the list as well: "Tear your hearts, not just your clothes, and return to the Lord your God. For he is gracious and compassionate, slow to anger, abounding in faithful love, and he relents from sending disaster" (Joel 2:13). And there are many more. Read Exodus 34:6, Numbers 14:18, Psalm 86:15, and Jonah 4:2, and you will find the same wording used to describe God's patience with His children.

You may find it interesting that, in Psalm 103:13, David considers the compassion of an earthly father and attributes this quality as a reflection of our heavenly Father: "As a father has compassion on his children, so the Lord has compassion on those who fear him." One meaning of *fear* is to "have a reverential awe of," such as to "fear God,"[5] showing honor and a sincere awareness of His formidable position and power. Fathers learn to lead their children with compassion by following God's example. His relationship with us is one based on both His compassion for us and our respect for Him.

The Lord Jesus compared earthly dads to our heavenly Father when He said, "If you then, who are evil, know how to give good gifts to your children, how much more will your Father in heaven give good things to those who ask him" (Matthew 7:11). If we as fathers model the heart of our heavenly Father to our sons and daughters, then they can flourish in a healthy way. What this looks like practically is following what I like to call "the way of grace."

The Way of Grace

I have long been asking myself, "What is a healthy family?" I have reduced my answer to this parenting definition and strategy: Through love and respect, healthy families overcome fear and shame by following the way of grace together. Let me explain what I mean through the following graphic.

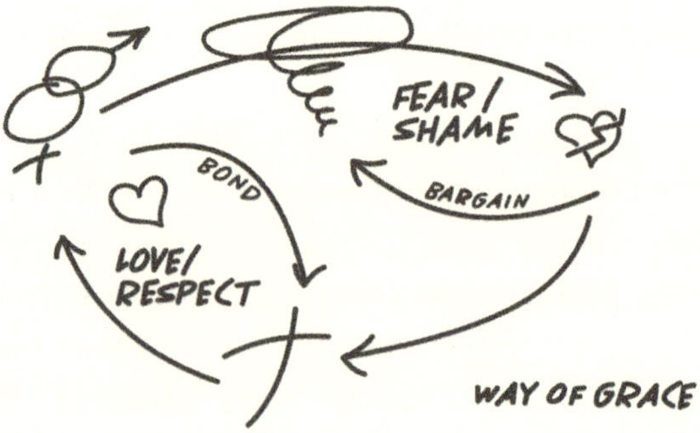

Focus on the top left corner of the infographic. God created the first man and then said, "It is not good for the man to be alone. I will make a helper corresponding to him" (Genesis 2:18). In creating Eve, God instituted marriage and established the structure of a family.

When sin entered the equation, the natural healthy version of relationships—with God and with one another—was broken. As the graphic shows, a cycle of fear and shame spun up as a result and wreaked havoc on human relationships, especially on how people communicate with one another. Our homes have been unhealthy ever since because our hearts have become hardened. Jesus warned about this hardening when the Pharisees questioned Him about divorce:

> Some Pharisees came to test him, asking, "Is it lawful for a man to divorce his wife?" He replied to them, "What did Moses command you?" They said, "Moses permitted us to write divorce papers and send her away." But Jesus told them, "He wrote this command for you because of the hardness of your hearts. But from the beginning of creation God made them male and female." (Mark 10:2–6)

Because sin hardens hearts, many Christian couples and families are stuck in the cycle of conflict. It's a story as old as Adam and Eve. Temptation leads to sin. Sin leads to shame and fear (as shown in the graphic). Shame and fear lead to bargaining (e.g., "If you do this, I'll do that" or "I won't do this unless you do that"), which leads not to love and peace but to fear and conflict. And from here, the cycle starts all over again.

Shame and fear became what our first parents modeled to their sons. Within one generation, jealousy led to anger, which resulted in Cain killing his brother, Abel. The cycle of fear and shame won that day. (You can begin to see why being a good father begins with having a healthy marriage.) But God intervened by making a way for us to be reconciled to Him and to one another. He made for us a way of grace. Through what Christ carried out on the cross, He made it possible for us to live in peace and harmony with Him and with one another. As the gospel takes root in our hearts, we are filled with the new life of God's Spirit. Now, we can "be kind and compassionate to one another, forgiving one another, just as God also forgave you in Christ" (Ephesians 4:32). As we practice redemptive conversations, our marriages will deepen into a mature covenant. Fathers and mothers will pass on the example of kindness and compassion to their children—and families will begin to experience the blessing of unity. Instead of a cycle of fear and shame, our homes will take on a culture of love and respect, reflecting what Paul wrote about in Ephesians 5:22–6:4:

> Wives, submit to your husbands as to the Lord, because the husband is the head of the wife as Christ is the head of the church. He is the Savior of the body. Now as the church submits to Christ, so also wives are to submit to their husbands in everything. Husbands, love your wives, just as Christ loved the church and gave himself for her to make her holy, cleansing her with the washing of water by the word. He did this to present the church to himself in splendor, without spot or wrinkle or anything like that, but holy and blame-

> less. In the same way, husbands are to love their wives as their own bodies. He who loves his wife loves himself. For no one ever hates his own flesh but provides and cares for it, just as Christ does for the church, since we are members of his body. For this reason a man will leave his father and mother and be joined to his wife, and the two will become one flesh. This mystery is profound, but I am talking about Christ and the church. To sum up, each one of you is to love his wife as himself, and the wife is to respect her husband. Children, obey your parents in the Lord, because this is right. Honor your father and mother, which is the first commandment with a promise, so that it may go well with you and that you may have a long life in the land. Fathers, don't stir up anger in your children, but bring them up in the training and instruction of the Lord.

By choosing God's redemptive way of grace, we can train our children to accept and extend forgiveness and to become "gracious and compassionate, slow to anger and great in faithful love" (Psalm 145:8).

Applying the Way of Grace

How does applying the way of grace work in real time?

At the time of this writing, our oldest daughter has graduated from high school and is preparing to enter college. As a dad, I find myself asking a million questions: "Is she ready?" "Will she make it in the big world?" "Did I do the job God gave me to do?" "Have I done all I can so far?"

Let's start by answering that last question honestly. No, I have not done everything I should have done. I think back to times when I've lost my temper, times when I've been selfish, and times when I've been wrong as a dad. But if I dwell on the times I've messed up and dropped the ball, shame and fear will creep in, telling me I need to manipulate the situation to "save face." Yet it's in these moments that I also remember that I can choose God's grace instead of letting fear and shame lure me into emotional bargaining. I remind myself that I can trust God despite being less than perfect as a dad. Shame and fear do not win; God's grace does. And choosing the way of grace in humility breaks the cycle of conflict, which leads to love and respect.

More than anyone else, my wife, Mandi, has taught me to see myself through the filter of God's grace. I am a survivor of the cycle of fear and shame because of God's grace. We all are. We are "more than conquerors through him who loved us" (Romans 8:37). If we choose to live in fear and shame, forgetting we are more than conquerors, then we end up allowing our past wounds to run our lives.

Every member of every family has wounds of the heart, some of which we are not even aware. These wounds—taking the form of insecurities, wrong beliefs, misunderstandings, and so on—become the source of the unhelpful, hurtful words and shameful actions that harm the ones we love. You've heard the old adage "Hurt people hurt people." Wounds of the heart can be healed only in healthy relationships, where we extend and receive forgiveness and build trust over time. This is what the way of grace is all about.

As we experience the love of Christ, a confident assurance begins to replace the old ways of anxiety and fear. John put it this way: "There is no fear in love; instead, perfect love drives out fear, because fear involves punishment. So the one who fears is not complete in love" (1 John 4:18). Slowly but surely, by God's grace, we will become better husbands and fathers. Our wives will become better in their roles as well. We are to influence and encourage rather than control and manipulate. And the modeling of compassion, kindness, grace, and forgiveness will be passed on to our children.

When Christ is present in our homes, we can have God's peace. Through the ups and downs of life, we can continually circle back to the gospel and humble ourselves with the message of the cross. Our wounds of the heart can be healed through Christ and through the healthy relationships we foster within our households. For "if anyone is in Christ, he is a new creation; the old has passed away, and see, the new has come!" (2 Corinthians 5:17). This illustration of the way of grace demonstrates the transforming work of the gospel: bringing forgiveness, redemption, and well-being to our families.

Living Wisely

As dads, God has called us to take the lead. We need to teach and train our families in the way of grace until it becomes the culture of our homes. This will help us to live well, with humility, ensuring that our "works are done in the gentleness that comes from wisdom" (James 3:13).

Our heavenly Father commissions us to model healthy relationships for our kids and how to navigate them during stormy seasons of interpersonal conflict. A friend of mine who has a ministry to families likes to say that Deuteronomy 6:4–9 is the Great Commission of the family's life together:

> Listen, Israel: The Lord our God, the Lord is one. Love the Lord your God with all your heart, with all your soul, and with all your strength. These words that I am giving you today are to be in your heart. Repeat them to your children. Talk about them when you sit in your house and when you walk along the road, when you lie down and when you get up. Bind them as a sign on your hand and let them be a symbol on your forehead. Write them on the doorposts of your house and on your city gates.

This certainly sounds like a worthy commissioning statement for fathers, doesn't it?

Jesus said, "My Father is glorified by this: that you produce much fruit and prove to be my disciples" (John 15:8). How we treat other people is one of the greatest tests for being a follower of Christ. As fathers, we want our kids to know God's will and to follow it, especially when it comes to loving and serving others. Teaching this to our children is part of our job as dads.

Paul gives us a remarkable command in Philippians 4:9: "Do what you have learned and received and heard from me, and seen in me, and the God of peace will be with you." Fathers, let us live out our faith in such a way that we can humbly say to our children, "Do as I say *and* as I do!" And may God turn your fatherly example into a reality for them.

To live out this calling effectively, we need the Lord's wisdom. I often pray for the wisdom God has promised: "But the wisdom from above is first pure, then peace-loving, gentle, compliant, full of mercy and good fruits, unwavering, without pretense. And the fruit of righteousness is sown in peace by those who cultivate peace" (James 3:17–18). As we seek God's wisdom and live in His presence, we will become peacemakers in our families.

Following the Way of Grace Together

Dads, where do we begin? Jesus said, "I am the way, the truth, and the life. No one comes to the Father except through me. If you know me, you will also know my Father. From now on you do know him and have seen him" (John 14:6–7). Christ Himself embodied the way of grace. Ask God to help you be known as a dad who is "gracious and compassionate, slow to anger and great in faithful love" (Psalm 145:8). Let Christ refresh your heart. He is the way to the Father, and He shows us who the Father is. The more time you spend with your heavenly Father, the better father you will be! Then make the most of every opportunity to spend quality time with your family.

Let me share an example from my childhood of what the way of grace can look like for a parent: When I was a child, my parents gave me a puppy one Christmas. Dad let me name the new dog, and it was the first time I felt the responsibility and joy of caring for another life. Eventually the day came when I lost my "best friend." I was heartbroken, and I attempted to hide my grief out of shame of what my family would think. But my parents supported me and helped me through my grief: My mother held me and stayed with me, and when my dad got home, he also stayed near. My parents responded to this difficult experience by showing me grace and comfort. They made me feel safe and secure.

In that tender moment, God began to teach me that life includes loss. Yet, despite this loss, I learned that with God's grace, I would never be alone.

My wife reminded me recently that the days are long, but the years are short. Seize each moment to be present and engaged with your children. Listen to their hearts and participate in their interests and activities. Let them see your genuine faith. This will compel them to follow Christ as well.

In closing, I have provided the following Scripture references for reflection as you seek to emulate Christ and model the way of grace to your family.

Scriptures for Reflection

> As the Father has loved me, I have also loved you. Remain in my love. If you keep my commands you will remain in my love, just as I have kept my Father's commands and remain in his love. (John 15:9–10)

> For you did not receive a spirit of slavery to fall back into fear. Instead, you received the Spirit of adoption, by whom we cry out, "Abba, Father!" The Spirit himself testifies together with our spirit that we are God's children, and if children, also heirs—heirs of God and coheirs with Christ—if indeed we suffer with him so that we may also be glorified with him. (Romans 8:15–17)

For I am persuaded that neither death nor life, nor angels nor rulers, nor things present nor things to come, nor powers, nor height nor depth, nor any other created thing will be able to separate us from the love of God that is in Christ Jesus our Lord. (Romans 8:38–39)

The grace of the Lord Jesus Christ, and the love of God, and the fellowship of the Holy Spirit be with you all. (2 Corinthians 13:13)

See what great love the Father has given us that we should be called God's children—and we are! The reason the world does not know us is that it didn't know him. (1 John 3:1)

Dear friends, let us love one another, because love is from God, and everyone who loves has been born of God and knows God. . . . Love consists in this: not that we loved God, but that he loved us and sent his Son to be the atoning sacrifice for our sins. (1 John 4:7, 10)

James Barham is a marriage and family counselor with Arkansas Baptist Children and Family Ministries. He and his wife, Mandi, have been married for 25 years. They have three children and several farm animals. James enjoys spending time outdoors with his family.

3

What It Means to Be a Man

TIM NOEL

I am amazed at how radically things have changed since I was a kid. My brother Jason and I were two tough dudes in our neighborhood when we were young. We grabbed our BB guns, jumped on our bikes, beat up the bad guys, and saved the girl! We pretended to be television show heroes who chased down bad guys, finding examples from *The A-Team*: Lieutenant Templeton Peck, Captain "Howling Mad" Murdock, and the legendary Lieutenant Colonel John "Hannibal" Smith. He was famous for saying, "I love it when a plan comes together!" We also mastered the expression, "I pity the fool" just like Mr. T said it in *Rocky III*. Back then, being a man meant something different than it does today.

Hollywood's Version

The social norms of an earlier era gave us a clear understanding of what it meant to be a man. Men were protectors; men got the job done; men overcame the odds to defeat evil. But this picture of manhood had been established long before Hollywood created fictional male characters on screen. Go back a couple of generations and consider how grandpas spun their family folklore:

> Did I ever tell you about your Uncle Bob? He was out cuttin' down a tree, and the saw jerked and cut deep into his thigh. Cool as a cucumber, he set the chainsaw down and limped to the house. He found your Aunt Carolyn's sewin' kit, stitched himself up, and headed back out to finish the tree work. His brother would string 40 acres of barbed wire, haul hay, put a new roof on the barn, and service the tractor all before breakfast, saying it had been a slow morning!

Those rough-and-tough guys would pick up a snake like it was just a tree branch. They were fearless.

Nowadays, however, the media is changing the definition of manhood. The traditional view of what it means to be a man is portrayed as oppressive and outdated, indicating that men shouldn't do things like string barbed wire or fix tractors anymore. They are now portrayed as needing to relinquish leadership and fashion themselves as kinder and gentler.

Ironically, these competing definitions of the acceptable man both fall short. As Christian fathers, we shouldn't take our cues from Hollywood's Mr. T or swallow the girl-power desire for a feminine man. Instead, we should take our directives from the Creator of men—from God Himself.

Let's look at the Word and see how God created manhood.

God's Version

In the Old Testament, we see dozens of examples of triumphant men: Abel, Enoch, Noah, Abraham, Moses, David. The list goes on and on. Sometimes, Scripture allows us to see one's growth from childhood all the way to his death as an old man. Take David, for example. We see him grow up from a boy to a man, then from a man to a warrior, then from a warrior to a king. Eventually, we hear God's commentary on David's life: He was "a man after my own heart" (Acts 13:22). Scripture gives us a fairly full view of David: We read of his slipups and failures, his battles and victories, and his repentance and restoration. In the Psalms, we bask in his beautiful portrayals of God's promises, but we also wallow in a fair amount of "woe is me" whining. Through it all, however, David seemed determined not to run away from bears, lions, or giants—or his own shortcomings, difficulties, and failures. He learned to face them head-on, and, in the process, he became God's version of a man.

According to God's Word, What Does It Mean to "Be a Man"?

Eventually, when David's life was almost over, he had an end-of-life conversation with his son. We read David's final instructions to Solomon in 1 Kings 2:1–4:

> As the time approached for David to die, he ordered his son Solomon, "As for me, I am going the way of all of the earth. Be strong and be a man, and keep your obligation to the LORD your God to walk in his ways and to keep his statutes, com-

> mands, ordinances, and decrees. This is written in the law of Moses, so that you will have success in everything you do and wherever you turn, and so that the LORD will fulfill his promise that he made to me: 'If your sons take care to walk faithfully before me with all their heart and all their soul, you will never fail to have a man on the throne of Israel.'"

David finished his life strong by placing on his son the responsibility to become a man of God. Let's break this passage down and hear the words of an aged father who got it right.

First, David accepted that he was not going to live forever. By examining his nearly completed life, we can conclude that David was a godly man, had become a successful king, and, with God's leading, had provided security and prominence for his kingdom. But David understood he was mortal. He was under the curse of death brought on by sin. Consider how he begins his parting advice to Solomon: "Be strong and be a man" (1 Kings 2:2).

1. BE STRONG

This sounds like something every dad has told his children: "Be strong. Stay tough. Hang in there. Don't give up." It is good advice. But notice David was not telling Solomon to go on a testosterone-driven rage in order to prove himself strong. His counsel was to be strong, not cocky. David had learned when he was young that human strength is drawn from God. We hear this lesson loud and clear from David during his battle with Goliath:

> Today, the LORD will hand you over to me. Today, I'll strike you down, remove your head, and give the corpses of the Philistine camp to the birds of the sky and the wild creatures of the earth. Then all the world will know that Israel has a God, and this whole assembly will know that it is not by sword or by spear that the LORD saves, for the battle is the LORD's. He will hand you over to us. (1 Samuel 17:46–47)

David didn't find the strength to defeat Goliath in himself; he had learned long ago—perhaps as a shepherd who defeated bears and lions—that man's strength comes from God.

Now, the wisdom of the aging David echoes in the future words of Paul: "Finally, be strengthened by the Lord and by his vast strength" (Ephesians 6:10). Being strong is a desire God gives to fathers. But let's be honest: The call to be strong requires wisdom, because the need to be strong tends to show up when times are scary—when the enemy lines up for battle, when giants appear and battle lines are drawn, when threats emerge with the intent of attacking the sheep God has called fathers to protect. Fathers must be strong, but not strong in the wrong way.

Think back to the strength David showed against Goliath. King Saul had thought strength was found in armor and weaponry—you know, in *human* strength. The young David knew that success against the giant would require *God* to propel the rock to Goliath's forehead. Therefore, when David urged Solomon to be strong, he defined the command with this caveat: "And keep your obligation to the LORD your God to walk in his ways and to keep his statutes, commands, ordinances, and decrees" (1 Kings 2:3). In other words, the call to be strong comes through the door of humility. God will empower us when we humble ourselves and "walk in his ways" (1 Kings 2:3).

It took me a while to learn this lesson. You see, when I was younger, I wasn't the biggest guy, so I was always trying to prove myself. I wanted people to see that I was strong, that I was a man! But I attempted to prove it in my own strength. You might say that I needed David to remind me that God is the source of my strength.

Take a moment to hear David's advice through Solomon's ears. His father, the king, was dying, and Solomon was the apparent heir. He would soon be crowned king of Israel. In short fashion, Solomon would lead a nation, and the coming responsibility would require strength to fill his father's shoes. He would need to stand firm against the opposition and protect the kingdom against an onslaught of enemies.

So will you, fathers! God has called you to be the gatekeeper for your family. He has called you to stand firm against enemies that threaten your wife and children. Make no mistake: "A thief comes only to steal and kill and destroy" (John 10:10). And, as Peter warned, "Your adversary the devil is prowling around like a roaring lion, looking for anyone he can devour" (1 Peter 5:8). But Peter outlined the winning strategy: "Be sober-minded, be alert. . . . Resist [the adversary], firm in the faith, knowing that the same kind of sufferings are being experienced by your fellow believers throughout the world" (1 Peter 5:8–9).

Do you get it? There is a very real Enemy among us, and God has called fathers to stand at their posts and protect their family.

Allow me to put this in easier terms. If you were camping with your family and a bear entered your campsite, you would defend your family at all costs. While you may not be camping right now or poised to fight a bear, our Enemy, the devil, is afoot. He is prowling in your family room and your kids' bedrooms. He may even be sniffing out his prey at your dinner table. He rides the bus with your children and walks the halls of their school. God has called you, as their father, to fight for your children, and Scripture gives us the following strategy:

> Finally, be strengthened by the Lord and by his vast strength. Put on the full armor of God so that you can stand against the schemes of the devil. For our struggle is not against flesh and blood, but against the rulers, against the authorities, against the cosmic powers of this darkness, against evil, spiritual forces in the heavens. (Ephesians 6:10–12)

Men, take to heart what Paul wrote: "Be strengthened by the Lord and by his vast strength," and you cannot be defeated!

2. PROVE YOURSELF A MAN

With strength as his first recommendation, David added this to his end-of-life counsel: "Be a man" (1 Kings 2:2). A great deal of confusion swirls in our society around what it means to be a man. To hear someone say "Be a man!" may turn heads and raise eyebrows. These adverse reactions may grow from the influence of humanism and modern feminism—and the many rotten examples of men who get it wrong. But deeper than the cultural influences that make "being a man" sound strange is the lack of biblical teaching on manhood. If you asked the Lord "What does it mean to be a man?," how would He answer? According to Scripture, being a man begins with growing out of childhood. Consider what Paul wrote:

> When I was a child, I spoke like a child, I thought like a child, I reasoned like a child. When I became a man, I put aside childish things. (1 Corinthians 13:11)

Paul meant that a time comes when we are to put away childish things. In David's message to Solomon, the context suggests the same. He was saying, "Solomon, you're about to take over my throne. Being a king is grown-up work, so it's time for you to start thinking like a man."

Reflect on how a typical child thinks. From their early years, children reveal they are born selfish through "Give me," "I want," "I need," or "It's mine!" statements. A child perceives the world they can see, a world they can comprehend and manage. A child thinks about small spaces—their homes, yards, neighborhoods, and so forth. A child sees short spans of time, measured in yesterdays and tomorrows. Children are small, so they think small. They create a comfort zone for themselves. And that's appropriate—*for a child*. But Paul calls godly men to mature beyond childish thinking. Therefore, we become selfless, generous, and servant minded. We sacrifice for the good of our children and others. Or, as Paul indicates, as we become adults, we learn to put an end to childish ways of thinking.

This is important enough that we need to let it soak in a little. As men, we need to expand our thinking from our comfortable worlds to a larger world with significant tasks to accomplish. We mature into understanding that God does not always call us to fun or comfortable or even manageable tasks. He may call us to things that stretch us, broaden our perspectives, or make us realize we cannot accomplish them without Him. For example, God has called you, as a father, to teach your children to believe in Him. You are given the sacred task of passing on the faith to the next generation. What a contrast to the small thinking that pursues a fun and comfortable environment. God calls all parents to the critical mission to share His Word:

> These words that I am giving you today are to be in your heart. Repeat them to your children. Talk about them when you sit in your house and when you walk along the road, when you lie down and when you get up. Bind them as a sign on your hand and let them be a symbol on your forehead. (Deuteronomy 6:6–8)

With a little imagination, you can see the difference between how a child reasons and how a man does. When a child chooses to do wrong, they rationalize it like this: "I've done something I wasn't supposed to do. It was wrong. But as long as Dad doesn't find out, everything is cool." You can boil down childish ethics to one line: "It isn't wrong if I don't get caught." But God calls us to put an end to childish thinking.

Be the father who stops trying to get away with wrong things. Be done with doing what you know is wrong because you know God is willing to forgive you—again. Live in the fear that you cannot pull anything over on the Father. He pursues you from behind and from ahead. He sees your every step, perceives your every thought, hears your every word, and sees your every action. When David challenged Solomon to "be a man," he was telling him to grow up and face an awful truth about sin—one David knew all too well: "For all have sinned and fall short of the glory of God" (Romans 3:23). It was David, after all, who faced his own demons when he confessed, "Against you—you alone—I have sinned and done this evil in your sight. So you are right when you pass sentence; you are blameless when you judge" (Psalm 51:4).

What I am trying to say is that being a man invites fathers to take responsibility for their actions, to see the big picture, and to realize God has a mission for them that begins with serving their wife and children.

David called on his son to be strong and to be a man. Then he put the jewel in the crown with the third piece of advice: "And keep your obligation to the Lord your God" (1 Kings 2:3). You can think of this as the answer to the question "How do I be strong and be a man?"

3. BE FAITHFUL

In a word, David was advising Solomon to be faithful. He knew the best way for Solomon to see the benefits of faithfulness was for him to examine models of faithfulness in other men. Notice how detailed David became when he fleshed out the call to be faithful:

> Be strong and be a man, and keep your obligation to the Lord your God to walk in his ways and to

> keep his statutes, commands, ordinances, and decrees. This is written in the law of Moses, so that you will have success in everything you do and wherever you turn, and so that the LORD will fulfill his promise that he made to me: "If your sons take care to walk faithfully before me with all their heart and all their soul, you will never fail to have a man on the throne of Israel." (1 Kings 2:2–4)

David had given godly advice to his son, but he had also given him so much more. He had provided him an example to live by. We hear God's assessment of David's faithful reputation stretching to the New Testament:

> [God] raised up David as their king and testified about him, "I have found David the son of Jesse to be a man after my own heart, who will carry out all my will." (Acts 13:22)

Godly examples of faithfulness speak volumes to our children. The Holy Spirit inspired the writer of Hebrews to provide a kind of "Hall of Fame" in Hebrews 11 for those who kept the faith. (Feel free to set this book down for a few minutes and read Hebrews 11.) Example after example fills the Hall of Fame for the faithful. By faith, Enoch did this. By faith, Abraham did that. And add Isaac, Jacob, Joseph, and so many others to this list as well. David made the list, of course, but the writer makes no reference to the slaying of Goliath or to David's musical prowess that produced dozens of psalms. Instead, kudos is given because David was "approved through [his] faith" (Hebrews 11:39). Every person who made the list in Hebrews 11 is commended for their faithfulness.

If we're honest, dads, don't we all want to be heroes to our children? We want to know they feel safe because we are stronger than their fears—because we'll provide for their needs and have the answer to their every question. Wanting to have a hero dad is as natural to our children as us wanting to be their hero.

That's how I feel. I want to be a hero to my children because my dad was a hero to me. Even as an adult, I still view my father as a hero. It's not because he always got it right. He is my hero because, throughout my 48 years of life, he has consistently been faithful to God. Sure, he misses the mark from time to time. Yet he has been, and continues to be, faithful. Faithfulness to God is the legacy my dad handed down to me and my brothers. And faithfulness is the legacy God desires for you to hand down to your children.

Being a mighty man of God is of high importance. To be faithful is what God has called us to do:

> Therefore, brothers and sisters, since we have boldness to enter the sanctuary through the blood of Jesus—he has inaugurated for us a new and living way through the curtain (that is, through his flesh)—and since we have a great high priest over the house of God, let us draw near with a true heart in full assurance of faith, with our hearts sprinkled clean from an evil conscience and our bodies washed in pure water. Let us hold on to the confession of our hope without wavering, since he who promised is faithful. (Hebrews 10:19–23)

Faithfulness to your heavenly Father will naturally overflow into faithfulness to the children God has called you to lead.

Conclusion

Being a man to your children should not tempt you to become like Mr. T or Rambo. Nor should you become the modern version of a passive Ken in Barbie's feminist world. Your pattern should come from God's Word—from the many examples of fathers and other men who found their strength in the Lord, found their manhood in obedience to God, and found the path they should walk in the Scriptures. Like Abraham, Moses, Daniel, and David, you won't always get it right. But with faithfulness to the Lord as your focus, you will leave a legacy worthy of a hero.

Tim Noel has served as the director of church partnership for Arkansas Baptist Children and Family Ministries in Little Rock, Arkansas, since February 2022. Prior to joining this ministry, Tim served as senior pastor of Trinity Baptist Church in Searcy, Arkansas, from 2011 to 2022. Tim has been married to Heather since 1999. They have three children: Eli, Abbi, and Evan.

4

Words from the Father: Three Things Every Child Needs to Hear

JEFF THOMPSON

About 17 years ago, back when my boys were young, I was traveling for the Great Commission Baptist Association, so I spent almost every Sunday in churches other than my own. From October until almost June, I was in out-of-town churches while my wife, Susie, and our boys worshipped in our church back home. As June approached, I marked Father's Day on my calendar, determined to worship with my family. I pulled it off, and God used that sermon to change me as a father.

My pastor invited us to turn to Matthew 17, and I thought, "The story of the Transfiguration . . . Hmm . . . I don't remember ever hearing a Father's Day sermon from this passage." But over the next hour, he preached in a way that opened my eyes. It altered how I viewed parenting and how I would relate to my sons.

Before the Transfiguration

Before I show you the specifics, a little scriptural context will help.

One chapter before the Transfiguration, Jesus asked His disciples, "Who do people say that the Son of Man is?" (Matthew 16:13). Peter nailed it with a line that has become famous: "You are the Messiah, the Son of the living God" (Matthew 16:16). Jesus's response was a watershed moment: "Blessed are you, Simon son of Jonah, because flesh and blood did not reveal this to you, but my Father in heaven. And I also say to you that you are Peter, and on this rock I will build my church, and the gates of Hades will not overpower it" (Matthew 16:17–18). That was a good day for Peter.

Many New Testament academics believe this moment was the turning point when Christ began to set his face toward Jerusalem, the city where He would surrender His life on the cross. It makes sense when you look at what follows. Jesus had spent two and a half years in ministry, but "from then on Jesus began to point out to his disciples that it was necessary for him to go to Jerusalem and suffer many things from the elders, chief priests, and scribes, be killed, and be raised the third day" (Matthew 16:21). And Peter—the one who just hit the homer by identifying Jesus as the Messiah—"took him aside and began to rebuke him, 'Oh no, Lord! This will never happen to you!'" (Matthew 16:22).

You know what's coming, right? Jesus had to get stern with His well-meaning disciple: "Get behind me, Satan! You are a hindrance to me because you're not thinking about God's concerns but human concerns" (Matthew 16:23). Jesus's passionate response reveals that He knew He was destined to die on the cross—and sooner instead of later. For the next six months, the intensity of His teaching and the opposition to the gospel weighed heavily on Him. This was a crucial time in the life of Christ.

About a week after the stern rebuke, Jesus led Simon Peter, James, and John "up on a high mountain by themselves" (Matthew 17:1). Here is Matthew's account of what took place on the Mount of Transfiguration, which the pastor preached about on that Father's Day:

> [Jesus] was transfigured in front of them, and his face shone like the sun; his clothes became as white as the light. Suddenly, Moses and Elijah appeared to them, talking with him. Then Peter said to Jesus, "Lord, it's good for us to be here. If you want, I will set up three shelters here: one for you, one for Moses, and one for Elijah." While he was still speaking, suddenly a bright cloud covered them, and a voice from the cloud said, "This is my beloved Son, with whom I am well-pleased. Listen to him!" When the disciples heard this, they fell facedown and were terrified. Jesus came up, touched them, and said, "Get up; don't be afraid." When they looked up they saw no one except Jesus alone. (Matthew 17:2–8)

Every sermon I had ever heard about the Transfiguration had gone in a similar direction. A preacher might say something like this: "On the mountain, God said, 'Look, I'm gonna let you catch a glimpse of My Son's glory. This story shows that Jesus Christ is fully God. It proves His divinity." Who could argue with a sermon like that?

But the pastor on this Father's Day went a different direction. He said,

> Even more than showing us the deity of Christ, this story shows us His humanity. Because, you

> see, Jesus was at that critical moment when He was turning from all the preaching, the teaching, the healing, the parables—all the ministry He'd been doing—and He was focusing on the cross. Jesus knew what was coming: the suffering and the mocking. The crown of thorns. Having His Father forsake Him. The disciples had no clue. But Jesus knew exactly what was coming. He was struggling with what lay ahead. We see the struggle again at Gethsemane when He cried out, "My Father, if it is possible, let this cup pass from me. Yet not as I will, but as you will" (Matthew 26:39). On the mountain, Jesus needed Father God's affirmation. And it came in these audible words: "This is my beloved Son, with whom I am well-pleased. Listen to him!" (Matthew 17:5)

As I sat in the pew with my family, my eyes were opened to this moment in Matthew 17 when God the Father was giving needed encouragement to His Son.

Three Things Communicated by God the Father

On the Mount of Transfiguration, Jesus needed to be with His Father. With the Savior's focus locked on the coming crucifixion, Jesus needed to hear from Him. And God the Father spoke to Him clearly.

The words of our heavenly Father are messages every son or daughter needs to hear from their earthly fathers as well. They are a balm to a child's soul. They are life giving. They inspire the courage to persevere. This realization impacted me as I worshipped with my family on that Father's Day morning.

As I listened to the sermon, I was struck by the irony of the parenting crisis of our modern world.

- Worldwide, about 7 percent of children grow up in a single-parent household. In the majority of these households, the father is the one who's absent.[6]
- In the United States, this number jumps to 23 percent.[7]
- Even in homes where fathers are present, the average time a father spends interacting with his kids in direct conversation is 30 minutes per week.[8]
- Contrast 30 minutes with the 40 to 60 hours a week that the average child will spend on a screen—gaming, texting, watching movies, scrolling through social media, and so forth.[9]

The next generation craves affection, affirmation, and approval—and too often, these essential human needs are not being met by their fathers.

Let's read again what the Father said to Jesus: "This is my beloved Son, with whom I am well-pleased. Listen to him!" (Matthew 17:5). In short, the three things the Father communicated to His Son were words of affection, words of affirmation, and words of approval.

WORDS OF AFFECTION: "THIS IS MY BELOVED SON"

When the voice from the cloud said "This is my beloved Son," the heavenly Father was essentially saying three words that our children need to hear: "I love you." For some of us dads, saying affectionate words just isn't our style. We'd rather *show* love than *say* it.

As a product of the state of Oklahoma, I know the classic tough-guy response when you ask a husband if his wife knows he loves her: "I told my wife I loved her when we got married. If it changes, I'll let her know." If you're one of those guys, let me speak in terms you might understand: That's a load of horse manure! Our wives and our children, the people we love, need to hear us say that we love them. I know this because I learned it the hard way.

I grew up as the baby of my family. My older brother, Johnny, was nine years old when I showed up by surprise. He wasn't too happy to relinquish his title, partly because he suddenly had to share his bedroom with me. As we grew up, he was pretty tough on me. He never said, "I love you." After all, what older brother tells a younger sibling stuff like that? But I knew he did.

Eventually, when we were both grown, married, and having kids of our own, it was clear we loved one another. But by my mid-30s, I could count on one hand the number of times either one of us had actually said it to each other. More often, we communicated it in our actions. I gave my son Hunter the middle name of Johnny, after my brother, and Johnny gave his boy the first name of Jeffrey, after me. We loved each other, but we just didn't feel the need to say it out loud.

In time, Susie and I were serving as missionaries in the Philippines. We'd been gone for six months when I got an email from my sister, Cindy, that said, "Johnny passed out on the floor and was throwing up blood. He's in the ICU. Talk soon." Man, I started burning up the phone lines, but I couldn't get ahold of anybody for three days. By the time I made a connection, Johnny was fine. Turns out he had a bleeding ulcer. He had passed out from the loss of blood. Once they figured out what it was, they were able to get him squared away. But the terror of thinking he might have passed away changed both of us.

When Susie and I flew home, Johnny was waiting for us at the airport. When we met him, he looked at me and said, "Hey, man—I love you, Jeff." You could have knocked me over with a feather. The first words out of his mouth were words of affection. But that's only part of the story.

As it turns out, the morning when Johnny passed out, he and his son Jeff had been arguing—the kind of verbal free-for-all that ended with a slamming door as Jeff stomped off to school. When Jeff came home that afternoon, he found his dad passed out with blood all over the floor. It freaked Jeff out. All he could think about was the fact that the last thing his dad heard him say was "Fine!" as he slammed the door earlier that morning. That moment signaled a shift in Johnny and Jeff's relationship. Johnny told me, "Jeff won't leave the room I'm in until I tell him that I love him."

Listen, if my brother Johnny, who is as mean and curmudgeonly and manly as any tough guy from Oklahoma, can learn to say "I love you" in public, so can you. His moment of crisis changed him, and it signaled a shift in our relationship too. Now "I love you" are words—not just actions—we share freely.

We could have learned the need to express affection more easily from what God the Father said to Jesus on the Mount of Transfiguration: "This is my beloved Son."

The pastor of the Father's Day sermon continued to the second thing God the Father said to his Son, through words of affirmation.

WORDS OF AFFIRMATION: "WITH WHOM I AM WELL PLEASED"

On the mountain, God added words of affirmation to His words of affection. He was essentially saying, "I love you and I'm proud of you."

Every child needs to be affirmed. The voice in their head is asking questions like these:

- Do I measure up?
- Do I matter?
- Is my dad proud of me?

Fathers, your kids need to know that you love them and that you are proud of them. You see, inside our children's minds, they know they do some things well, but they also know the areas in which they've messed up. This mixed bag of success and failure leads children to ask, "Is my dad's love dependent on me being good enough?" "Is my dad proud of me?" These questions begin in adolescence but will echo into their adult years.

When I was in the seventh grade, I was introduced to the weird world of mathematics. Math and I didn't get along too well, especially in algebra. I mean, what evil force came up with a system where you add letters together instead of numbers?

On my first big test, I scored a 36—not a 36 out of 40, mind you, but a 36 out of 100. Test scores that bad came with a consequence: a required parent signature indicating my parents had seen my score. My dad, who can look at a roof and calculate its slope and say "That'll take four square . . ." was not going to be happy with me when he picked me up from school. When I got in the car, Dad greeted me in the normal way he always did.

"How was school today, Jeff?"

"OK," I said, hoping he'd accept my vague answer.

"How'd your tests go?"

"OK," I lied.

I hadn't figured out yet that when your dad is a preacher, vice principals will call and tell them things that you don't even know they're telling them. Dad already knew my "OK" was a deflection strategy.

Finally, he put me out of my misery: "Let me see your math test." When I gave it to him, he looked at my 36 out of 100 and asked, "Is that the best you can do?"

How do you answer a question like that? I mean, 36 was a bad score, and I was bad at algebra, but I didn't think I was "36 percent" bad.

"I could've done better."

All of a sudden, I broke down. I don't know why, but the little 12-year-old version of me let out the waterworks. At 12 years old, you're not supposed to cry, even if you get hurt. But I was bawling.

My dad looked at me and said, "Why are you crying?"

And it all came out: "Because you're going to hate me! You won't be proud of me!"

At that moment, my dad let me in on a little secret that many 12-year-olds may not know. He said, "Whoa! You think that my being proud of you is determined by math? Jeffrey Will, I am proud of you because you are my son. If you do your best, I'll always be proud of you."

A huge burden was lifted from my shoulders. I don't remember a time before that when my dad had ever told me he was proud of me simply because I was his son and not because of what I did. I started to believe it that day, but it wasn't until my own son was born that I realized what it meant to be proud of someone simply because they're yours.

Just as your children need to hear you say "I love you," they also need to hear you say "I'm proud of you."

When the Father spoke to Jesus on the Mount of Transfiguration, He was offering words of affection and affirmation. But that's not all: His message that day also contained words of approval for His Son.

WORDS OF APPROVAL: "LISTEN TO HIM!"

The third part of the Father's message was that of approval: "Listen to him!" Essentially, God was saying, "I love Jesus, I'm proud of Him, and His words are My words."

Your children need to know they have their father's approval. They need assurance that their father approves of who they are and of the good things they're doing, knowing that you believe in them and that what they think matters.

As you read this part, you might have the same thoughts I had during the Father's Day sermon: "Of course the heavenly Father approves of *His* Son. Jesus is the Messiah! My children are great—but they are not divine!"

Face it. There will be times when your kids disappoint you. Their attitudes, words, and actions will break your heart. But there will also be times when they get it right, and when they do, it's important to get excited for them. When they grasp something, cheer them on. When they are tenacious through difficulty, compliment them. When they are kind, give them a verbal standing ovation. Whenever they share willingly with others, especially without your prompting, pour words of affirmation on them.

Allow your words of approval to flow freely, even for the little victories you observe. Let me show you what I mean by using two of my young grandsons, Judah and Zion, as an example. Judah and Zion are cousins. As the oldest, Judah rules the roost. To a toddler, roost ruling means that sharing things doesn't come easily. One day, Zion was throwing his normal "I don't want to take a nap!" tantrum. (I mean, Zion would scream and cry at every nap time. He had such a strong will!) He had cried so much that his eyes were red and puffy, and little Judah decided to do something about it. He toddled over to the baby bed, pulled the pacifier out of his own mouth, put his arm through the slats, and offered his pacifier to his cousin to try to help him calm down.

I watched with amazement. As the king of his young kingdom, Judah was never fond of sharing. But when he heard his cousin crying, he decided to remedy the problem. I was so proud that I could have thrown a parade in his honor. Small victories like this may seem simple, almost silly, yet they present teachable moments through which we can let our children know we approve of their actions.

Words of affection, words of affirmation, and words of approval. Until that Father's Day sermon so many years ago, I had never stopped to consider that the Transfiguration would transform my parenting strategy. But it did.

On the Mount of Transfiguration, the heavenly Father spoke words of affection, words of affirmation, and words of approval over Jesus—and He did so in an audible voice. It was just what the Son of God needed to hear. In His humanity, Jesus received from His Father the words our children need to hear from us:

- I love you.
- I am proud of you.
- You got it right!

Maybe you grew up like I did. Maybe your dad didn't tell you that he loved you or that he was proud of you or that he noticed you got it right very often. Or maybe it's worse than that. Maybe your dad walked out and left your family. Please hear me loud and clear: Whatever your experience—even if you've never heard those words from your earthly father—if you're a believer, then the same Father from whom Jesus heard those words is also saying them to you. Because, you see, God says "I love you" to each of us.

Jesus put it clearly in the most familiar verse in the Bible: "For God loved the world in this way: He gave his one and only Son, so that everyone who believes in him will not perish but have eternal life" (John 3:16). And that's not the only mention of God's love for us in Scripture. There are dozens of verses recorded in the Bible that tell us this.

When I was in elementary school, my Sunday school teacher told me that putting my name in place of "the world" in John 3:16 would help me see how personal God's love is: "For God loved Jeff in this way . . ." And I urge you to do the same. It will help you know that He loves *you*. That He is proud of *you*. That He notices when *you* get it right and when *you* are speaking His gospel. Isn't that what Acts 1:8 says? "But you will receive power when the Holy Spirit has come on you, and you will be my witnesses in Jerusalem, in all Judea and Samaria, and to the ends of the earth." He loves you. He's proud of you. And He wants you to tell the world about Him.

Follow the Father's lead. Tell your children often that you love them. Let them hear the words "I'm proud of you" flow freely from your lips. And let them know that you have confidence in them to do what is right. Loud and proud—that's the pattern the heavenly Father left for us when He said, "This is my beloved Son, with whom I am well-pleased. Listen to him!" (Matthew 17:5). God's example will change the way you father your children, just like it changed me.

That Father's Day sermon rocked my world. From that day forward, my boys heard words of affirmation every night at bedtime, and even now, as adults, they can't leave a room or hang up the phone without my saying "I love you" or "I'm proud of you" or "You nailed that one, son!" Why did that sermon impact me so much? That's an easy one: If the Son of God, the second Adam, needed to hear those words from His Father, then my kids need to hear it from their father as well.

Jeff Thompson has served as associational missions strategist for the Great Commission Baptist Association in Fort Smith, Arkansas, since October 2007. He has been married to Susie since January 1990 and is the proud father of his two sons, Hunter and Tyler. His sons are married to Lorrel and Ashleigh, the best daughters-in-law ever. Jeff and Susie have five grandchildren: Anna, Judah, Zion, Shiloh, and Adelaide. Jeff also serves as a trustee of the Arkansas Baptist Foundation.

5

How to Be a Bad Dad

CRAIG JENKINS

As you can see from the title of this chapter, I'd like to talk about what it means to be a "bad" father. While the title may have taken you by surprise, sometimes looking at examples of what *not* to be as dads makes it easier for us to see what kind of dads we *should* be, according to God's purpose for us.

Have you heard about the dad who was playing cops and robbers in the backyard with his three energetic boys? One of the bandits popped out and fired two rounds in the direction of his dad. "Bang! Bang! You're dead, Dad!"

In dramatic fashion, the dad put on an award-winning performance: He slumped to his knees. The pistol fell from his limp hand. He dropped to the ground, his eyes closed and his body unmoving. When he didn't move for several minutes, the next-door neighbor got worried. He hurried to the crime scene and bent over the victim. The overworked father opened one eye and whispered, "Shh! Don't give me away! This is the only chance I've had to rest all week."

This story made me laugh the first time I heard it—partly because I could relate to it. However, I soon realized an important truth that will apply to many fathers: We have to stop playing dead as dads.

The Bible has more than a few examples of bad dads: Jacob had a blind spot in loving Joseph as a favorite, and this led to a strained relationship between Joseph and his brothers (Genesis 37:3–4). Eli the priest struck out because he honored his sons more than he honored God by allowing them to continue to serve in the temple, even though they did not know the Lord and defiled His house (1 Samuel 2:12–36). David didn't discipline his children very well, and his focus on the kingdom and not his kids may have contributed to his son Absalom leading a rebellion against him (2 Samuel 15) and his son Amnon being involved in a scandal with his half sister (2 Samuel 13). Then there is Lot, Abram's nephew. He offered to let the evil men of Sodom do whatever they wanted to his daughters. Let's admit it: Lot may stand as the best example of what *not* to do as a father. That's right—the episode from Genesis 19 wins him the notorious title of the worst dad in the Bible.

Let's learn from Lot about what not to do.

To Be a Bad Dad . . .
Ignore Potential Consequences

Before we can get to what happened in Genesis 19, we need to explore how Lot got there.

Lot and Abram were kinfolk. They had made the journey from their home in Haran to the land of Canaan that God had called Abram to. In Genesis 12 we read how the journey begins.

In Genesis 13, we read that the flocks and herds of Abram and Lot were too much for the land to support, so

Abram came up with a solution. Instead of their herdsmen fighting over pastures and water, Abram decided it was best to split up. He approached Lot and gave him the first choice, saying, "Separate from me: if you go to the left, I will go to the right; if you go to the right, I will go to the left" (Genesis 13:9).

Lot looked out over the land and decided on the lush area of the Jordan Valley:

> Lot . . . saw that the entire plain of the Jordan as far as Zoar was well watered everywhere like the Lord's garden and the land of Egypt. . . . Lot chose the entire plain of the Jordan for himself. Then Lot journeyed eastward, and they separated from each other. Abram lived in the land of Canaan, but Lot lived in the cities on the plain and set up his tent near Sodom. (Genesis 13:10–12)

Lot based his choice on what seemed best for him at that moment. Who wouldn't pick the fertile, lush land of the Jordan? Unfortunately, he failed to consider the people in the eastern cities and how their influence might affect his family. His decision eventually proved fatal.

The Bible says that Lot "journeyed eastward" (Genesis 13:11). According to *The Complete Word Study Old Testament*, the Hebrew word translated "east" is often used as a geographic direction. The word also carries the meaning of being either good or bad. The word references the location of Eden being east (good) and also references the habitat of the men who built Babel being to the east (bad).[10]

Like Lot, we can fall to the appeal of pursuing the promises of the lush river valley lifestyle. A promotion at work may mean less time for our kids' activities. Moving into an expensive house may put a strain on the budget, preventing family vacations. Purchasing a lake house for "family fun" each weekend may become an alternative to Sunday worship as a family.

Bad dads fail to think through the long-term consequences of their decisions. Good dads think ahead, using wisdom to consider the possible outcomes.

To Be a Bad Dad . . .
Treat Spiritual Things Lightly

By the time Genesis 19 rolls around, Lot is steeped in the consequences of his decision to go east. Clearly, Lot's thinking has been influenced by the evil culture that surrounds him. The Lord sends messenger angels to warn Lot of the impending destruction that is coming to Sodom:

> The two angels entered Sodom in the evening as Lot was sitting in Sodom's gateway. When Lot saw them, he got up to meet them. He bowed with his face to the ground and said, "My lords, turn aside to your servant's house, wash your feet, and spend the night. Then you can get up early and go on your way." (Genesis 19:1–3)

It's hard to grasp whether Lot realized who these men were. Did he react this way because he knew they were angels, or was he just being hospitable? We cannot be sure from the text. What we can be sure of is that he convinced them to stay in his home, not the town square. He cooked a meal for them, and they ate together. On the surface, it seems that Lot was doing a nice thing, but let's look at this passage more closely.

Lot has these spiritual beings in his home, and they give him instructions to leave Sodom—once after dinner and then again the next morning—but he does not take them seriously. Their warning is crystal clear, but so is Lot's dismissive negotiations with them:

> "Run for your lives! Don't look back and don't stop anywhere on the plain! Run to the mountains, or you will be swept away!" But Lot said to them, "No, my lords—please. Your servant has indeed found favor with you, and you have shown me great kindness by saving my life. But I can't run to the mountains; the disaster will overtake me, and I will die. Look, this town is close enough for me to flee to. It is a small place. Please let me run to it—it's only a small place, isn't it?—so that I can survive." (Genesis 19:17–20)

The angels warn Lot about what is coming for Sodom, and they tell him to warn his family. But Lot ignores the warnings. Worse than that, he negotiates a compromise when they tell him to flee. Lot would rather go to the nearby city of Zoar.

It's easy to see Lot's errors yet be blind to our own. Too many fathers today act just like him. They invite spirituality into their lives by making time for daily devotions and being involved in church. But when God speaks a word of warning through a verse they read, a sermon they hear, or a nudge from the Holy Spirit, they dismiss it. They fail to take the word seriously. They fail to repent from sinful thoughts or turn off a TV show when it crosses a line. They join others in complaining about something or gossiping about someone from church or work. They negotiate a lesser amount of tithes and offerings, justifying an ungrateful heart for the things God has given.

Ignoring the nudges of the Lord and the conviction of the Holy Spirit is the perfect recipe for being a bad dad. It's crucial that you take the things of God seriously, listening to the wisdom and the warnings He gives you.

To Be a Bad Dad . . .
Handle Attacks Alone

If you have ever wondered why God destroyed Sodom, the scene on Lot's porch should provide the answer. The depth of perversion in Sodom hung like a stench among multiple generations. From the old to the young, the people were brazened. The porch scene played out this way:

> Before [Lot and the angelic visitors] went to bed, the men of the city of Sodom, both young and old, the whole population, surrounded the house. They called out to Lot and said, "Where are the men who came to you tonight? Send them out to us so we can have sex with them!" (Genesis 19:4–5)

This city is forever known for the act of sodomy.

The tension rises as the Sodomites seek to satisfy their evil desires—to have sex with the angelic visitors. Lot joins them on the porch in an attempt to turn them away. The scene escalates as they press hard against Lot and try to break down the door. Lot is completely overwhelmed. By himself, he is ineffective in stopping this attack.

I don't know which is more disturbing: the mob's attempted attack on Lot, his home, and his guests or the ignorance Lot shows by believing he can handle a matter of this magnitude alone. Genesis 19:10–11 reveals the angelic rescue:

> But the angels reached out, brought Lot into the house with them, and shut the door. They struck the men who were at the entrance of the house, both young and old, with blindness so that they were unable to find the entrance.

Unable to see, the perverted men tire themselves out and leave.

Don't miss the point here: Lot could not defend his home alone. God's supernatural intervention is what turned the outcome of the spiritual attack in Lot's favor! How, then, does this story apply to you? Satan is attacking your family and home, and he's doing so brazenly. Jesus made it clear, saying, "A thief comes only to steal and kill and destroy" (John 10:10).

Bad dads believe they can repel a spiritual attack on their own. Being a good father means asking the Lord to help you when such an attack comes.

To Be a Bad Dad . . .
Sacrifice Your Children

At the beginning of this chapter, I went out on a limb in accusing Lot of being the worst dad in the Bible. I'm ready to show you why. With the evil men surrounding his house, Lot goes outside and offers them a plea bargain that goes like this:

> He said, "Don't do this evil, my brothers. Look, I've got two daughters who haven't been intimate with a man. I'll bring them out to you, and you can do whatever you want to them. However, don't do anything to these men, because they have come under the protection of my roof." (Genesis 19:6–8)

This is all the proof you need to see that Lot wins the notorious title of the worst father in the Bible.

There's no way to sugarcoat this. Lot was willing to offer his daughters for sex to the mob—willing to send his daughters deeper into the wickedness of this perverted city. Honestly, this makes me mad. Some may think he is a jerk, a bum, and an unfit father. It's hard not to vilify Lot for willingly offering to sacrifice his daughters to those agents of evil. What kind of dad would do that?

Sadly, it happens all the time.

Dads, do you know what kind of music your kids are listening to? Do you know the lyrics? Do you know what they are watching on TV? Do you know the websites they are browsing? Do you know what's being said or texted on their cell phones? Have you checked their Instagram or Snapchat or TikTok accounts? Do you know the friends they hang out with?

The Enemy is standing on your porch, pounding on the door. Your job is to protect your family, not to negotiate with the forces of evil.

Bad dads act like Lot. They see the wolf outside and open the door. Good dads protect their family, doing all they can to avoid such an attack in the first place.

To Be a Bad Dad . . .
Ignore a Situation's Urgency

Through God's intervention, Lot's daughters do not become victims of the lecherous mob, but Lot doesn't suddenly see the error of his ways. The angels make it clear that their visit to Sodom is not social; it is business. They are there to rescue Lot and his family from the impending destruction of Sodom and Gomorrah (Genesis 19:12–13). Because of Lot's family connection to Abraham, God is willing to warn Lot and give him an opportunity to escape. But he fails to take the warning seriously. We see Lot's reluctance play out over the next 12 hours:

> So Lot went out and spoke to his sons-in-law, who were going to marry his daughters. "Get up," he said. "Get out of this place, for the Lord is about to destroy the city!" But his sons-in-law thought he was joking. At daybreak the angels urged Lot on: "Get up! Take your wife and your two daughters who are here, or you will be swept away in the punishment of the city." But he hesitated. (Genesis 19:14–16)

Sure, Lot goes to his sons-in-law to warn them. He even uses an exclamation in his plea, but the manner and tone of his warning was not very convincing. I mean, the sons-in-law thought he was joking. Daybreak reveals that even Lot doesn't seem convinced. He continues to hesitate. Finally, by the grace of God, the angels grab Lot and his family and rush them out of the city.

Lot lacked a sense of urgency. He figured that Sodom would still be standing the next day. He was hesitant to heed the angels' warning and felt no need to act quickly.

For some bad dads, a lack of urgency is their go-to strategy. They keep banking on having time to invest in their home "later on." They think tomorrow is the day to get involved in their kids' lives, not today. In reality, there is never a better time than the present to turn from your Sodom and run to the hills!

Bad dads refuse to feel a sense of urgency when it's needed. Good dads heed the warning, head to the hills, and refuse to look back.

To Be a Bad Dad . . .
Reject God's Help

Dragged away by the two angels, Lot and his family made it out of the city before its destruction—all except his wife, who turned into a pillar of salt because she longingly "looked back" at the city she was losing (Genesis 19:26).

We also know that this intervention was not the first time that God had rescued Lot. Back in Genesis 14, Lot was among the Sodomites who were taken as prisoners of war by four area kings and their armies. When word got to Abram that his nephew had been imprisoned, Abram marshaled 318 warriors and set out to rescue them. They pursued the captors from south to north, caught them, defeated them, recovered both people and possessions, and headed back to Sodom.

How ironic that, after having been rescued by God in chapter 14, Lot has grown complacent by chapter 19. He has squandered the lesson of God's help. I wish I could tell you that Lot finally learns his lesson—that the worst is behind this notorious dad. But because of the final scene of Genesis 19, I can't. I'll summarize and then let the words of Scripture tell the full story.

Lot and his daughters end up living in the mountains instead of in the nearby village of Zoar. His two daughters realize that their fiancés—the ones who laughed off Lot's warning about Sodom's impending doom—did not survive the firestorm. Now without prospects of starting a family, they hatch a wicked plot that goes like this:

> The firstborn said to the younger, "Our father is old, and there is no man in the land to sleep with us as is the custom of all the land. Come, let's get our father to drink wine so that we can sleep with him and preserve our father's line." So they got their father to drink wine that night, and the firstborn came and slept with her father; he did not know when she lay down or when she got up. The next day the firstborn said to the younger, "Look, I slept with my father last night. Let's get him to drink wine again tonight so you can go sleep with him and we can preserve our father's line." That night they again got their father to drink wine, and the younger went and slept with him; he did not know when she lay down or when she got up. So both of Lot's daughters became pregnant by their father. (Genesis 19:31–36)

The firstborn daughter gave birth to Moab, who is still known today as the father of the Moabites. The younger daughter gave birth to Ben-ammi, who is still known today as the father of the Ammonites (vv. 37–38). Both sons became enemies of Israel, God's nation and people.

How tragic that Lot squandered God's intervention in his life. God protected, preserved, and rescued Lot, yet instead of learning from God's intervention, he wasted the opportunity. And the fruit of his life didn't fall far from the tree.

Bad dads squander God's help, as Lot did. Good dads acknowledge God's help and learn from their mistakes. Has God moved in your life? Has He rescued you from difficult situations? Has He forgiven you, restored your fortunes, and led you out of trouble by the hand? If so, don't ignore His faithfulness or what He is trying to teach you. Instead, learn from the past and choose to walk with Him more closely. Don't worry about guarding the status quo; don't close your eyes and play dead. Keep your eyes open and seek the Lord's help when an attack comes.

In other words, it's time to man up as a dad!

Craig Jenkins serves on the executive team of the Arkansas Baptist State Convention as the director of convention advancement and news. A native of Fort Worth, Texas, Craig graduated from Ouachita Baptist University and Southwestern Baptist Theological Seminary. He is married to Melanie and is the proud dad of three sons: Ryan, Reid, and Rett. Craig and Melanie have one daughter-in-law, Gracie, and a grand-dog, Honey. Before beginning his service to the Arkansas Baptist Convention in 2021, Craig served as a pastor in Texas and in Arkansas for 30 years.

6

Dads Make a Difference

BOBBY CLARK

In the Old Testament, we read the story of a young Jewish woman named Esther (or Hadassah). Her story is set in Persia, formerly Babylon, the captor of the nation of Judah. The narrative picks up at a time when many Jews had returned to Jerusalem, while others remained in Persia. The book of Esther is the only biblical record from the perspective of the exiles who stayed behind in Persia.

Mordecai, one of the exiled Jews, plays a significant role in this story. We don't know what his job was or if he married and had children of his own, but we do know this: Like Esther, he did not return to his homeland. He stayed in Persia and adopted Esther, his younger cousin, who had lost both her parents and who is described in Scripture as having "a beautiful figure" and as being "extremely good-looking" (Esther 2:7).

It may seem odd to use the story of an orphaned child in a book about fatherhood, but we'll be considering Mordecai's role as Esther's father figure and the role he played in the events that took place.

What Mordecai Can Teach Us About Fatherhood

GOOD FATHERS DON'T JUST HAPPEN

Good fathers aren't the result of chance. There's more to being a father than biology. Mordecai was not Esther's father. He wasn't an uncle or even an older brother who became the man of the house when Esther was orphaned. As her older cousin, Mordecai made a choice to step in and raise her as his own. That's what good fathers do: They decide to step up to the plate and fulfill their calling as a father. And Esther's situation called for the wisdom and support of a father figure.

In the first chapter of Esther, we read that King Ahasuerus became angry with Queen Vashti and removed her from her royal position. By the time chapter 2 rolls around, we read that a search was launched across the empire and that Esther, who "had a beautiful figure and was extremely good-looking" (Esther 2:7), was selected as a finalist to replace the deposed queen. This is where Mordecai's fatherly instincts first became apparent:

> Esther did not reveal her ethnicity or her family background, because Mordecai had ordered her not to make them known. Every day Mordecai took a walk in front of the harem's courtyard to learn how Esther was doing and to see what was happening to her. (Esther 2:10–11)

Just as a father gives wise counsel to his daughter, Mordecai gave Esther wise advice and checked in on her well-being.

And his fatherly oversight didn't stop there. In the year that followed, Esther received beauty treatments and eventually had a second audience with the king. Scripture reveals that Esther had "obeyed Mordecai's orders, as she always had while he raised her" (Esther 2:20). But the stakes of her uncle's role were elevated by the end of chapter 2. Mordecai had uncovered a plot to kill the king, and he passed this information on to Esther, who told the right people and saved the king's life. Scripture sums it up like this:

> When the report was investigated and verified, both men were hanged on the gallows. This event was recorded in the Historical Record in the king's presence. (Esther 2:23)

The first fatherly insight buried in Esther's story is that good fathers aren't "good" automatically. Good fathers are men like Mordecai who take action when needed—who step up to the plate, act with integrity, and seek their children's welfare. In Esther's case, Mordecai gave wise counsel and kept an eye on her, intervening when necessary.

GOOD FATHERS MODEL GOOD CHARACTER

This leads to a second fatherly insight from Esther's story. In the Scripture, we read of Haman, a raging bigot with an oversized ego who had it out for the Jews. Elevated to Persia's second-in-command, "the entire royal staff at the King's Gate bowed down and paid homage to Haman" (Esther 3:2). But Mordecai, who was also present at the gate, refused to bow down. He would bow to God and God alone, and this enraged Haman.

Get ready for one of the greatest fatherhood lessons out there: Character is caught more than it is taught. Your children watch you like a hawk. They watch how you respond in difficulty. They listen to your words. They see your values in action. And then they absorb your actions and make them their own.

I'll make my point by jumping ahead in the Esther narrative, showing how the Mordecai-versus-Haman story played out. In time, Esther went on to demonstrate a significant amount of courage in an effort to save her people, the Jews. Where do you think she learned to be courageous? Where did she learn to stand up when the stakes were high? It came from watching Mordecai. And this principle is revealed: A crisis doesn't create character—it reveals it.

Consider Mordecai's character both in his refusal to bow to Haman and during what resulted. Out of spite for Mordecai's defiance, Haman convinced King Ahasuerus to issue a decree to kill all Jews. The city of Susa panicked. Mordecai grieved, fasted, and prayed. To see how this crisis unfolded outside the palace walls, read what happened when Esther heard about the crisis and notice its impact on her:

> When Mordecai learned all that had occurred, he tore his clothes, put on sackcloth and ashes, went into the middle of the city, and cried loudly and bitterly. He went only as far as the King's Gate, since the law prohibited anyone wearing sackcloth from entering the King's Gate. There was great mourning among the Jewish people in every province where the king's command and edict reached. They fasted, wept, and lamented,

> and many lay in sackcloth and ashes. Esther's female servants and her eunuchs came and reported the news to her, and the queen was overcome with fear. She sent clothes for Mordecai to wear so that he would take off his sackcloth, but he did not accept them. Esther summoned Hathach, one of the king's eunuchs who attended her, and dispatched him to Mordecai to learn what he was doing and why. So Hathach went out to Mordecai in the city square in front of the King's Gate. Mordecai told him everything that had happened as well as the exact amount of money Haman had promised to pay the royal treasury for the slaughter of the Jews. (Esther 4:1–7)

Esther had a front-row seat to the teachable crisis. She observed her father figure model courage in crisis. Is it any wonder she developed into a courageous woman? As I said before, character is caught more than it is taught.

That doesn't mean that good fathers rely only on their actions to do the talking. Mordecai demonstrated character, then he used words to make sure Esther understood:

> If you keep silent at this time, relief and deliverance will come to the Jewish people from another place, but you and your father's family will be destroyed. Who knows, perhaps you have come to your royal position for such a time as this. (Esther 4:14)

The character Mordecai demonstrated in his fatherly role gave him the platform to point out the providential purpose of her life "for such a time as this." And this is the third fatherly insight we gain from a man who stepped into the paternal role: Mordecai challenged Esther to rise to her God-given purpose.

GOOD FATHERS CHALLENGE THEIR CHILDREN TO LIVE FOR A PURPOSE

Fathers, are you training, equipping, and encouraging your children to become who God has called them to be? Don't just tell your kids to chase their dreams—exhort them to live out their God-given purpose. Train them to walk in their God-given calling, not to seek worldly ambition.

Unlike Mordecai's fatherly influence on Esther's life thousands of years ago, yours is still being written. A reminder of what Esther grew up to become may encourage your efforts.

Finishing the Story

Encouraged by Mordecai, Esther stepped up to the plate and approached King Ahasuerus, even though doing so uninvited could result in death. However, God was with Esther:

> As soon as the king saw Queen Esther standing in the courtyard, she gained favor with him. The king extended the gold scepter in his hand toward Esther, and she approached and touched the tip of the scepter. "What is it, Queen Esther?" the king asked her. "Whatever you want, even to half the kingdom, will be given to you." "If it pleases the king," Esther replied, "may the king and Haman

> come today to the banquet I have prepared for them." The king said, "Hurry, and get Haman so we can do as Esther has requested." (Esther 5:2–5)

Haman received the royal invitation with delight. But his smile faded when, before the festivities, he once again encountered the defiant Mordecai. Encouraged by his wife and friends, Haman decided to take his revenge. He ordered gallows to be built to silence Mordecai once and for all.

That night, the king couldn't sleep. He called for the court records—the very ones that mentioned the incident where Mordecai had exposed an assassination plot years earlier. The following morning, the king asked Haman how he would honor someone who served the king well. Haman thought the king wanted to honor none other than himself, so he suggested dressing the recipient in royal robes and parading him through town on a royal horse. The king approved of this—and ordered Haman to arrange the parade for Mordecai. Haman was humiliated.

Haman's humiliation, however, was far from complete. At the banquet, Esther exposed Haman's plot to kill her people. Enraged, the king ordered Haman to be hanged on the very gallows he built for Mordecai. Through Esther's courage in approaching the king and revealing Haman's plot, she fulfilled the purpose God had intended for her.

Three Truths for Fathers

1. NEVER UNDERESTIMATE THE PROVIDENCE OF GOD

Fathers, some of you have a Haman in your life—something trying to destroy your family. It may or may not be a person. It may be a problem, a sin, or a situation. Don't give up, and don't underestimate God's providence. God has not revealed the final scene, and I assure you that gallows await your Haman. God is faithful, and He will preserve your family.

2. NEVER UNDERESTIMATE THE INFLUENCE OF A GOOD FATHER

Your job as a father is to keep sowing seeds of faith. Be loving and caring—but also be firm. Stand your ground based on biblical values, not on modern culture or trends. Whether your children are young or grown up, continue to influence them intentionally, and do not underestimate this influence.

3. NEVER UNDERESTIMATE WHAT GOD HAS IN STORE FOR YOUR CHILDREN

Esther was an exile who had lost both her parents—yet God used her to save a nation. What I'm saying is that each of your children has a God-given purpose that is greater than your wildest dreams for them. Teach them to pursue their God-given calling. Equip them to follow God's path. Encourage them to seek His will. Their natural, worldly instinct may be to run from it, but your encouragement, equipping, and training over the years will help them get where they need to be.

I should warn you: God's ordained purpose may not be the one you have envisioned. The willingness to push your children to discover what God has for them may be a learning curve for you. It was for me. When my oldest son was barely born—as soon as the umbilical cord was cut—I took him in my hands and held him over my head to the nurse's dismay. I prayed out loud, "God, may he be a messenger to his generation." At the time, because God had so radically saved my life, I was looking forward to my son being a preacher. But God had a different plan. God raised him up to be a doctor—to serve and save people through medicine, not pulpit ministry. Here's what I learned: We should never underestimate what the Lord has in store for our children.

Closing

Fathers, your influence matters more than you may know. God has called you to shape destinies and leave legacies for your children. Like Mordecai, be willing to bend your knee to God and God alone, to give your children wise counsel boldly, to watch over them, and to intervene when necessary. And remember: God has prepared you for such a time as this.

Bobby Clark has served as senior pastor of Abbott Baptist Church in Mansfield, Arkansas, for 27 years. He is also the chairman of the board of trustees for Camp Siloam and currently serves as the interim executive director. Bobby and his wife, Pennie, are blessed with three children: Dr. Joshua Clark and his wife, Jessica; Sarah Pope and her husband, Michael; and Bobby Clark Jr. and his wife, Whitney. Bobby and Pennie are also proud grandparents of five: Caleb, Madeline, Eleanor, Samuel, and Annalee.

7

Fulfilling Our Role as Fathers

TRAVIS MCCORMICK

If someone were to ask me what raising children is like, I think I would compare it to a construction project, with God as the architect and fathers as the construction managers.

Think about it. The architect establishes the design, and the construction manager oversees the construction project, communicating what each of the contractors needs to do to finish the project correctly, according to the architect's design. In the same manner, a father's job is to follow God's blueprint for helping his children grow into the people God has designed them to become. With that said, let's decipher part of God's blueprint instructions from Proverbs 22:6:

> Train up a child in the way he should go; even when he is old he will not depart from it. (ESV)

Two directives seem clear from this verse: 1) Train your child in the way he should go and 2) know what that way is. Training your child in this way—God's way—will help you fulfill your responsibility as a father, completing the project God has entrusted to you.

Train Your Children in the Way They Should Go

The first part of this verse clearly defines a father's role. A father is not called to design a career path for his children; rather, his role is to train them up in the way they should go. The Hebrew word translated "train up" can also be translated as "dedicate." Fathers are to dedicate their children to the Lord and then follow His plan and purpose. But as a father, doing so first requires you to follow God's purpose for your own life. This allows you to set an example for your children by helping them see that God's Word is real and practical for living life to the fullest.

When you embrace your God-given role as a father, a burden is lifted. It's not up to you to determine who your children should be. You don't need to worry if your plan is good enough, because you aren't called to follow your own plan; you're called to follow God's plan. The pressure comes off as you realize the fatherhood role begins by surrendering the process to the Lord. Your children are first and foremost His children, made in His image.

"Made in His image" means that God has created each child uniquely for His purpose. Your children are not like cookie-cutter houses in a suburban neighborhood. Each one is custom designed—"remarkably and wondrously made" (Psalm 139:14). Each has a unique combination of God-given talents, passions, spiritual gifts, interests, and personalities. And the individual collection of these custom features falls into God's individualized plan for each of their lives.

The father's role is to read the blueprint—to discern and follow God's plan for the children he is called to bring up. A wise father must learn to trust God's plan fully, even as his children grow up and make their own choices. This may be difficult, as it calls you to submit to being the construction manager, not the architect.

Know the Way Your Children Should Go

Second, as a father, you will find it easier to train your child "in the way he should go" if you know which way that is. In other words, you must know God's design in order to show it to your children. This requires you to communicate with the architect, study the blueprint, and oversee the process as the building takes shape. Let me explain these three activities in more detail.

COMMUNICATE WITH THE ARCHITECT

> *Make your ways known to me, Lord; teach me your paths. Guide me in your truth and teach me, for you are the God of my salvation; I wait for you all day long. (Psalm 25:4–5)*

As an earthly father, you have the privilege of praying to your heavenly Father. God invites you to talk with Him, and He promises that if you ask anything in His name, He will do it (John 14:14). And He promises that "if any of you lacks wisdom, he should ask God—who gives to all generously and ungrudgingly—and it will be given to him" (James 1:5).

So, ask the architect. Who better to talk to than the one who designed the blueprint? Ask Him to reveal His plan so that you can build according to His design.

READ THE BLUEPRINT

All Scripture is inspired by God and is profitable for teaching, for rebuking, for correcting, for training in righteousness, so that the man of God may be complete, equipped for every good work. (2 Timothy 3:16–17)

Discerning God's plan also requires serious examination of Scripture. Along with praying, you must read the Bible and trust the Holy Spirit to guide you. The Bible is the ultimate resource God uses to reveal both His plan and His purpose.

OBSERVE THE PROCESS

I will praise you because I have been remarkably and wondrously made. Your works are wondrous, and I know this very well. (Psalm 139:14)

The psalmist reminds us that each of us—parents, grandparents, and children—is uniquely made by a creative designer. But the psalmist teaches us to do more than notice this; we should also "know this very well." In other words, we discover God's design for our children by watching them and talking with them and spending time with them. By doing so, we begin to understand the specific ways God has "remarkably and wondrously" made them.

What are their likes and interests? What is their sense of humor like? How do they handle different situations? How do they interact with people? What do you notice about their personalities? What are their natural talents and abilities?

As construction managers who fulfill the architect's design, fathers will see the building of their children taking shape. This allows us to praise Him along the way for the beauty of His design.

In time, as your children mature, you can help them discover their God-designed gifts and tendencies through a personality test or a spiritual gifts inventory. At the very least, your relationship with your children will be strengthened as you show interest in who they are becoming. At best, you will become better informed and equipped to train your children to devote their lives to God's purpose.

Follow God's Way

As mentioned earlier, training your children in God's way doesn't mean laying out a career path for them. Your calling as a father is simply to be faithful in bringing up your children in His way and modeling what His Word says. In time, you will see God's plan unfold, but your responsibility day by day is to help your children grow into godly men and women. That said, Scripture presents the following guidelines to help you fulfill your role as a father.

TEACH GODLY CHARACTER, NOT JUST GOOD BEHAVIOR

> *Take off your former way of life, the old self that is corrupted by deceitful desires, to be renewed in the spirit of your minds, and to put on the new self, the one created according to God's likeness in righteousness and purity of the truth. (Ephesians 4:22–24)*

Getting your children to behave properly is not enough. The problem with "acting" the right way is that it may be just an act. If you look only at surface behavior, you may believe that your children are growing in God's design. But just because they are compliant doesn't mean they have godly character. God considers one's character by looking at the condition of their heart. He doesn't want your children *to pretend to be* righteous. He wants to change them from the inside out so they *actually are* righteous. Paul's challenge reminds us of the end goal: "To put on the new self, the one created according to God's likeness" (Ephesians 4:24).

MAKE GOD'S GLORY YOUR GOAL

> *So, whether you eat or drink, or whatever you do, do everything for the glory of God. (1 Corinthians 10:31)*

If you are going to raise your children to become all that God has designed them to be, then you need to help them strive for the goals He has set for them. This means teaching them to glorify God in everything they do. When this becomes their focus, life is about so much more than following rules and being "good." I encourage my children to ask this question all the time: "How am I bringing God glory in what I'm doing right now?" Teaching them to do everything for God's glory increases the likelihood that they will grow to resemble God's blueprint design for them.

ENCOURAGE ENDURANCE

> *Consider it a great joy, my brothers and sisters, whenever you experience various trials, because you know that the testing of your faith produces endurance. (James 1:2–3)*

This final guideline is one of the hardest lessons to prioritize in my own life, let alone to teach my children. It's the call to endure. As fathers, we want to protect our children from trials. We want them to be successful. We want them to achieve their dreams—with limited resistance.

At the same time, we know from Scripture and our own life experience that endurance does not come easily. Endurance is learned by persevering through difficulty. In practical terms, when we allow our children to quit something simply because it is hard, they may miss out on an opportunity to grow. They may be left wondering what could have been. Fathers must help their children learn to endure if they are going to grow into the people God designed them to be. That's what James teaches: "And let endurance have its full effect, so that you may be mature and complete, lacking nothing" (James 1:4). When our children endure through difficulty, they ultimately become more like Christ.

Complete the Project

Train up a child in the way he should go; even when he is old he will not depart from it. (Proverbs 22:6 ESV)

Solomon's guidance for fathers predicts a beautiful outcome. Remember, though, that this verse is a proverb, not a promise. Its intention is not to guarantee the outcome of a father's instruction but to give him wise advice. Although this guidance encourages fathers to embrace their role and follow God's plan, children still have free will and can choose to go their own way. However, if you do your part and dedicate your life to God and His perfect design, your children will have a higher probability of growing into disciples who make other disciples. In other words, a father's faithful efforts will help his children fulfill their purpose. Through these efforts, we "complete the project" the Lord has entrusted to us—that is, the directive to oversee and steward the upbringing of our children.

It's easy for fathers to misinterpret Proverbs 22:6 as an iron-clad promise: "If you get them started on the right path by taking them to church and teaching them about Jesus, they will love the Lord until the day they die." Sadly, we know this isn't always the case. Some children fail to commit themselves to Jesus—even children whose parents faithfully brought them to church and taught them His Word.

Involvement in a Bible-believing church may not guarantee that our children will walk with the Lord later in life, but raising them this way is essential for showing them the right path. Scripture teaches the importance of committing to a local community of Christ followers for the purpose of accountability and spiritual growth. At church, you worship, pray, praise, give, serve, study, and fellowship together. Yet, while church involvement is essential, it's just one component of helping our children become who God has designed them to be. While an important part of His plan, Jesus's command in the Great Commission (Matthew 28:19–20) is to make disciples, not perfect church attenders. Making disciples is our God-given purpose. And just in case you're wondering, you can tell you've made a disciple when they start making others into disciples as well. This is part of God's plan for your children.

If you believe that God has uniquely created your children and that He designed them to become disciple makers, then you must believe that He intends for them to use their gifts, talents, personalities, and passions for that purpose.

We have always been a sports-oriented family. All three of my children were born with natural athletic abilities and a passion for just about anything involving a ball. From an early age, they played on various teams through the city recreation leagues. They also played in Upward Sports (a Christ-centered sports program) and Boys and Girls Club programs, among others. Travel ball became a part of our lives when our son James was nine years old. A group of parents was wanting to get their boys together to start a travel baseball team and asked if James could join them. At first we refused, because we knew this commitment would take us away from our church during part of the summer. But we never really felt a peace about our decision. As a family, we began praying and talking it through, including James in the decision-making process. Eventually, we came to believe that God had provided this opportunity and that James's involvement on this team would be a way for us to practice what we preach about being disciple makers. We wanted our children to be known this way and not just as "pastor's kids," so, seeing this team as an opportunity for that, we signed him up.

James would be playing baseball to become the disciple maker God had designed him to be. As his father, it was my job to teach him how to use his gifts and passions to reach other people with the gospel, people who shared his athletic passion.

Our decision to support James included sacrifices of both time and money. It also made us the object of friendly fire from well-meaning church members who questioned our commitment to Jesus. They thought we had let our priorities slip because we were giving a lot of our time to sports. But God used our family as we interacted with other baseball families. Mostly, God used James to influence others. God also used the traveling team opportunity to teach James that while disciple making is difficult and comes at a price, it's worth it in the long run.

Speaking of the long run, fast-forward to the present. After years in baseball, basketball, volleyball, and soccer, my children have learned an important discipleship lesson: God gave them their talents and passions to impact the lives of the people around them. Now, they are deeply connected to their local churches. They have grown to love God and trust Him more as they've learned to use their influence as disciple makers. Let me show you what I mean.

At the time of this writing, my daughter, Reagan, teaches physical education and coaches junior high girls' basketball. Reagan's journey with basketball taught her perseverance. She's overcome more than her share of obstacles chasing her dreams. She's learned to rely on God. Because of that, she has developed a passion for influencing middle school girls in two roles: She serves as their leader at church and also coaches them at school. She loves basketball and Jesus, so she has put the two together.

My youngest son, Luke, exceeded expectations in his soccer and football career. He earned a walk-on spot at a Christian college and went on to be part of a national championship team. Luke impacted his teammates with his infectious love for God.

And our traveling team baseball player? Well, James earned the title of tournament MVP along the way to winning the high school state championship in baseball. God built this kid to play baseball! He was able to pursue his dream to play in college for two years. Unfortunately, due to an injury that sidelined him for his junior and senior seasons, he was not able to continue his playing career. However, instead of throwing in the towel, James took up the role of mentoring and ministering to his teammates during that time. He now attends Cross Theological Seminary in Rogers, Arkansas, where he is also an intern for the church's CTHREE college ministry. He works with all types of students, but he uses his athletic story to reach athletes. Not long ago, he led a hockey player to Christ and had the honor of baptizing him.

I hope that no one reading this thinks that I am advocating for the pursuit of passions over a commitment to God's church. Make no mistake, as someone who's been actively involved in church and denominational ministry for more than 35 years, I firmly believe that one must be connected to a local body of believers in order to become an effective disciple maker. My wife and I passed this belief onto our children, who grew up as active participants in the church and were raised to love the Lord with all their heart, soul, mind, and strength.

At the same time, we have seen firsthand the value of making our children into disciples who are disciple makers and not just church attenders. Having adult children who love the Lord and the local church is the culmination of where it all began. They have a burden for the lost, are committed to God and His mission, and their faith has become their own.

He Who Has Ears to Hear, Let Him Hear

Whatever the ages of your children, keep fulfilling your role as a father. Train them. Dedicate them to the Lord and remember these words from Jesus: "He who has ears to hear, let him hear" (Matthew 11:15 ESV). Let's use *HEAR* as an acronym to flesh out Jesus's command and apply it to our role as fathers.

- **H: Humans aren't perfect.** By God's design, everyone involved in your child's life is human. All of them—even the most loving, kind, and well-meaning people—will sometimes get it wrong. Our worldly heroes in sports and movies will stumble. Our heroes of the faith will reveal their flaws. So will pastors, youth workers, grandparents, and yes, even parents. We aren't doing our children any favors when we hold their influencers to an unattainable standard of perfection. We know that no one is perfect, yet we are often unwilling to cut people (ourselves included) any slack. Influencing children is an imperfect science, and we need to leave room for grace.

  This holds true for our children as well. We must recognize that they are not perfect either, which means they will mess up as well. We do our children a disservice when we foster unfair expectations of them. We need to imitate the actions of Jesus as He discipled His followers. He knew they would fail. And when they did, Jesus restored them. We should do the same thing for our children.

(It's important to note that while forgiveness and restoration is always the goal, there are some "mess-ups" that are far more serious than others and require further consequences and actions. Any form of abuse—sexual, mental, emotional, or physical—must be dealt with and immediately reported to the proper authorities. Follow-up must be done to prevent further abuse and to ensure the safety and well-being of any victim.)

- **E: Expect mess-ups.** Because all people are imperfect, we can expect all people to mess up. Scripture tells us that "all have sinned and fall short of the glory of God" (Romans 3:23). It's not a matter of *if* but of *when*. Take the apostle Peter, for instance. He was originally named Simon until Jesus changed his name to Peter, which means "rock." He played a prominent role in leading the early church and authored two books in the New Testament. He became part of Jesus's inner circle and yet was later addressed as "Satan" by Jesus Himself. Further failings occurred when Peter rebuked Jesus, cut off the servant's ear, and ultimately denied Jesus three times. The point is that Peter was a godly man, but he wasn't perfect. Even he messed up. No one is immune to mistakes. Knowing this and refusing to hold our children to an impossible standard of perfection will help save us from a lot of disappointment.
- **A: Admit mess-ups.** How we respond to inevitable mess-ups—our own and our children's—will go a long way in helping our children become all

God designed them to be. When you mess up, avoid rationalizing the mistake away. Admit you were wrong instead of pretending it never happened. When someone else blows it, be careful to avoid extremes in your response. One extreme is acting like the error is no big deal. The other extreme is treating it like the end of the world. Inevitable mess-ups become opportunities for mentoring and forgiveness. Take the example of Peter. He wasted a lot of time trying to avoid the truth but ultimately came to the point where he took responsibility for his actions and openly confessed to the Lord what he had done. We can learn a valuable lesson from him. When mess-ups happen, don't waste precious time denying the truth; seize the moment and admit the mistake instead.

- **R: Repent and move on.** Both parts of this equation are critical. Repentance is stopping in our tracks and accepting that we were heading in the wrong direction. It involves an admission of wrong. But repentance also implies a change of direction—leading to movement in the right direction. Peter came to the point of repentance. As a result, he received forgiveness, was restored to a right relationship with God, and continued to be used by Him in building His church.

My family experienced our own mess-ups in athletics. As much as we planned to use our experiences on the baseball field, the soccer field, or the basketball court as opportunities to make disciples, there were times when we failed to fulfill this mission. The problem wasn't that we tried and failed; it was that we sometimes failed to try.

There were times when we forgot why we were there and lost sight of our purpose, getting caught up in the excitement or disappointment of the moment. We spent some weekends simply playing/watching ball games. When this happened, the temptation was to make excuses, to give ourselves a pass, or simply to act like nothing was wrong. But we knew if we were going to be successful in the long term, we had to confess our mess-up as parents the same way we expected our children to come clean if they messed up. The goal of repentance isn't simply to forgive and forget but to learn from our mistakes and do better the next time. You see, repentance is humbling and yet freeing at the same time. When we teach our children to repent, we help remind them of who God is and who they are in Him.

Conclusion

God never promised that a father's job would be easy. The weight of shaping our children's hearts and leading them to become like Christ often comes with struggles, doubts, and moments of exhaustion. But as fathers, we are reminded that we're not in this alone. When Jesus commanded us to make disciples, He also promised He would be with us always (Matthew 28:19–20). As the construction manager in this most important building project, we must trust and depend on the architect for everything we need to complete the job He's given us. While the journey may be difficult, we are called to do our part—modeling Christlike behavior and praying for, teaching, and guiding our children along the right path. Ultimately, it is God who transforms their hearts, builds their lives, and brings the fruit of our labor. By trusting in Him and remaining faithful to fulfilling our role, we can help raise our children to become all that God has designed them to be.

Travis McCormick has served as the men and boys missions strategist at the Arkansas Baptist State Convention since July 2008. He has been married to Teresa for 29 years, and they have three adult children, Reagan, James, and Luke, and an amazing daughter-in-law, Ally. God has blessed Travis with the privilege of leading his children to faith in Christ and helping them become the men and women God designed them to be.

Endnotes

Chapter 1

1. Stephen Davis, in interview with the author, March 15, 2025.
2. Davis, interview.
3. Charles Haddon Spurgeon, "A Happy Christian," sermon, The Spurgeon Center, accessed July 15, 2025, https://www.spurgeon.org/resource-library/sermons/a-happy-christian/#flipbook/.

Chapter 2

4. A. W. Tozer, *The Knowledge of the Holy* (HarperOne, 2009), 1.
5. *Merriam-Webster Dictionary,* "fear," accessed August 8, 2025, https://www.merriam-webster.com/dictionary/fear.

Chapter 4

6. Stephanie Kramer, "U.S. Has World's Highest Rate of Children Living in Single-Parent Households," Pew Research Center, December 12, 2019, https://www.pewresearch.org/short-reads/2019/12/12/u-s-children-more-likely-than-children-in-other-countries-to-live-with-just-one-parent/.
7. Kramer, "U.S. Has World's Highest Rate."
8. Clifton Chadwick, "Seven Minutes a Day: The Modern-Day Excuse for a Parent," *The National,* November 13, 2011, https://www.thenationalnews.com/lifestyle/comment/seven-minutes-a-day-the-modern-day-excuse-for-a-parent-1.459183.

9. David Rosenberg and Natalia Szura, "Teens Are Spending the Equivalent of a 40-Hour Work Week on Their Devices: Here's How to Help Them Find the Right Balance," *Fortune Well*, October 24, 2023, https://fortune.com/well/2023/10/24/teens-too-much-screen-time-find-balance/.

Chapter 5

10. Spiros Zodhiates, *The Complete Word Study Old Testament: Bringing the Original Text to Life*, ed. Warren Baker (AMG Publishers, 1994).

Made in the USA
Coppell, TX
24 March 2026

74015291R00069